1-12. 2-2

W9-DII-566

CARL NIELSEN
CENTENARY ESSAYS

CARL NIELSEN

CENTENARY ESSAYS

Edited by
JÜRGEN BALZER

DENNIS DOBSON

LONDON

© *Nyt Nordisk Forlag — Arnold Busk A/S 1965*
Musical examples drawn by Thoria

Publication subsidized by The Cultural Foundation

First published in Great Britain in 1966
by Dobson Books Ltd., 80, Kensington Church Street, London W8
Printed in Denmark by Bianco Luno, Ltd. Copenhagen

CONTENTS

SOME PERSONAL REMINISCENCES

by

Thorvald Nielsen

I came across Carl Nielsen's name for the first time when I was a lad of eleven. The son of an artisan, I spent my childhood in the island of Falster. One dark winter evening I was sitting in my home in the glare of the kerosene lamp, reading the latest issue of "Aller's Familie Journal"—a very popular magazine among farmers and artisans in those days. Suddenly my eye fell on a picture with the text: Carl Nielsen, the famous composer of "Saul og David". I gave a start for I had even then decided on a musical career, and it flashed through my mind: Shall you ever meet that man when you come to Copenhagen? This secret wish did come true four years later when I received an invitation from my benefactor, Rolf Viggo de Neergaard, proprietor of the estate of "Fuglsang" in Lolland, to have breakfast with him at the Phoenix Hotel in Copenhagen. At the same time Mr Neergaard informed me, "I have also asked Carl Nielsen, for I want you to meet him, and him to hear you play the piano composition you have prepared for the entrance test to the Academy of Music." Naturally I turned up early; we sat down, I somewhat excited for I was already an ardent admirer of Nielsen's music, after I had recently heard him conduct his own "Maskarade" at the Royal Theatre. This was in the autumn of 1906.

At long last the door was opened by a short, agile, thickset man with brushed-back hair and a pair of large, greyish blue, twinkling eyes that dominated all his face. To my surprise and joy Carl Nielsen proved to be a plain and straightforward man; he spoke with a slight Funen accent, and I noticed his dark, manly voice. He adressed me in an extremely kind, almost charming manner, "So you want to become a musician and study at the Academy of Music." I don't remember anything more until we had finished the coffee and gone into the adjacent room where there was a piano. "Let us hear what you intend to play." Slightly anxious I played what I had prepared: the first movement of Beethoven's Sonatina in F major. He did not praise me, but said, "I, too, played a little composition at *my* audition before entering the Academy of Music, and that was by Mozart" (Nielsen always inserted a slight t-sound when pronouncing this name —Motzart). Then he sat down at the piano and played all the first movement of the Sonata in C major. I was much impressed by it at that time, but above all I devoured his bearing with my eyes; he sat erect at the piano without batting an eye while playing. During my later acquaintance with Nielsen it was charac-

7

teristic of him never to wear his heart on his sleeve, though he contained a volcano of feelings.

Some years passed during which I followed his artistic career from a distance. After my first meeting with Nielsen I studied all the music from his hand that I could get hold of. The very first work I made myself thoroughly acquainted with was "Saul og David"; this opera gave me the key to his peculiar mode of expression so that I never since had any difficulties in understanding his music.

In the year 1908 there was a change in Nielsen's circumstances. Already while he held the position as second violinist in the Royal Theatre Orchestra he had conducted the orchestra on several occasions, for instance at the performances of his own operas. In this field, too, his talent had attracted attention. So when the position as First Conductor became vacant at Johan Svendsen's retirement, Nielsen was invited to succeed him, and in 1908 he was appointed Conductor Royal. Three years before it had been possible for him to resign from his post as second violinist in the orchestra. This office, which he had been in charge of for 16 years, had often troubled him—being bent on other and greater things as he was. There was, however, one man at the theatre who did what he could to make life easier for Nielsen—*Johan Svendsen*. I have been told by an old colleague that during the period when the composition of "Saul og David" was in progress Svendsen quite often indicated to Nielsen with a motion of his hand before the last act of an opera or a ballet that he might go home now and carry on with his work. This outstanding Norwegian musician, composer, and conductor had an open eye for Nielsen's creative powers from the very first, and on every occasion he supported Nielsen with true greatness of mind in his struggle to gain a foothold as a composer.

Since the appearance of his earliest works Nielsen had met with continual criticism and lack of understanding in the press. Even some performing musicians failed to appreciate his music. An old violinist with whom I shared my music desk in the orchestra, once met my enthusiasm during a performance of "Maskarade" with these words, "Yes, but there is no melody, it is not tuneful." Even Fini Henriques, otherwise a great admirer of Nielsen, was overheard by me to say one evening after a concert performance of the second Violin Sonata, "By Jove, Carl, this is really mere affectation." He was talking about the pounding B flat that breaks in suddenly towards the end of the last movement. Nielsen, however, stuck unconcerned to his musical idea: without this B flat the end of the sonata would collapse like a house of cards.

The unique intensity manifested in Nielsen's musical ideas is thus the product of his condensed energy in working with melody and his understanding of the function of the interval in the thematic structure.

From the opening of the season in 1910 I played as a substitute in The Royal Theatre Orchestra, and this gave me the great experience of seeing Carl Nielsen on the platform frequently and of playing under his baton. There is no point in digressing on the various mean and personal pinpricks which Nielsen was exposed to inside the theatre during his time as conductor. I feel much more inclined to call to mind those great hours when his genius, also as a conductor, was so happily brought to full development. In my time I have played under many world-famous conductors, but no one has eclipsed the memory of, let alone surpassed Nielsen's performance of for instance "Don Giovanni", the Mozart symphonies in G minor and E flat major, and Schubert's "The Unfinished"; not to mention his own works—as a matter of course.

In the autumn I had become a member of Fini Henriques' string quartet. During a pause in a morning rehearsal the popular violinist and composer suddenly exclaimed, "By God, I feel like seeing Carl Nielsen, it's such a long time since we've had a chat. I think I'll call him up and ask him to come and have lunch with us." They lived five minutes' walk from each other, and this was no sooner said than done. The arrangement suited Nielsen, and he arrived; whereupon we regaled ourselves with a sumptuous repast. After lunch we withdrew to the music room with coffee and brandy. Fini, "Tell me, Carl, what are you doing at present?" Nielsen, "Well, as a matter of fact I'm working on a symphony." Fini, "Now, that sounds interesting, play something for us." Nielsen strikes up the opening bars of the "Espansiva" (see ex. 19, page 34). Fini starts up like lightning, "By Jove, Carl, this is the work of a genius." Nielsen, "You know, Fini, this theme is quite suitable for putting something up against" (a curious term for the concept of counterpoint). Then he showed by a number of examples how this might be done. I dare say that these glimpses from the "Espansiva" set the discussion going—time was no longer a reality—dinner came—evening came—midnight came—and we parted—I wonder when?

The work on "Espansiva" had been in progress for well over a year before it was finished on April the 30th, 1911. Another year was to pass before the first performance took place on the 28th of February, 1912, on which occasion the Violin Concerto got its original performance, too. Some days before we had the first orchestral rehearsal of the symphony in the rehearsal hall of The Royal Theatre. The orchestra had gathered, Nielsen sat down, gave the signal—and shot after shot thundered from the roaring orchestra with ever increasing rapidity as if to force out the theme—then it came. At this moment Nielsen turned pale—and sat up in his chair. We played the whole movement through without stopping. After the terrific orchestral storm and under the impression of the grandiose music, we all felt quite out of breath. Everybody realized that we had been present at a historic moment. And the concert at the Oddfellow Palace turned out a great triumph for Nielsen.

In the "Sinfonia Espansiva" Nielsen does not appeal to his audience by any studied elegance in the instrumentation. "I don't care for refinements," he once said—adding with a twinkle in his eye, "A harp in an orchestra is like a hair in a soup." But since David does play the harp, there was no avoiding it in "Saul og David". And it is true that he also admitted it in "The Mists Lift", the little lyrical piece for flute and harp in "The Mother". If anyone took Nielsen to task

9

with regard to the instrumentation of his works, he would cut them short, as in the reply he once gave to a close acquaintance who ventured a cautious criticism, "You know nothing about that—my instrumentation covers the content of my music completely." Similarly, I agree with Knud Jeppesen when he writes in an article in "Jyllandsposten": Carl Nielsen's instrumentation in particular has an aura of its own which is quite in harmony with the essence of the music—the purely spiritual content.

Nielsen's music does not aim at passive revelling in sweet harmonies, it aims at activating, stirring us. Another thing is that it also wants to give us rest. After the violent tensions that arise when the latent forces in the very idea of the music are released towards the climax, we are led into an Arcadia where the soul can relax in blissful peace, so to speak—but only to gain new strength.

One evening in the spring of 1912 after a performance at the theatre conducted by Nielsen, I heard his voice from the top of the stairs leading down to the room where our instruments were stored. "Is Thorvald Nielsen there?"—"Yes." —"Oh, would you care to walk home with me and have a little chat on the way." So we met outside the theatre. We had to walk in the same direction, down Strøget, to get to our homes; I lived at the north end of Vestervoldgade at that time, whereas Nielsen lived in Vodroffsvej. He asked me, to start the conversation I suppose, what I spent my time on, apart from the music. Well, I went into the reading room of the Royal Library whenever I had time for it. What I read there? Mythology, and at the moment I was reading "The Spiritual Life of the Norsemen" by C. A. Rosenberg. Rosenberg's name acted as an 'open sesame'. He became lively all of a sudden: "How very interesting; I, too, have read this excellent book." It is worth mentioning in this connection that while he studied at the Academy of Music Nielsen had spent some of his happiest hours in the home of the Rosenbergs, where he associated with the gifted sons and not least with the daughter Margrethe, in whom Nielsen had a true, lifelong friend. Perhaps we went on talking about mythology, I don't remember, but I accompanied him right to his home, and we took leave at the garden gate.

It fell to my lot quite often after this that Nielsen pounced upon me after a night's performance when he was in the mood for a chat. Truly inspired artist that he was, Nielsen had an inexhaustible creative imagination. On our way home one frosty night under a canopy of twinkling stars, our talk turned to Johann Sebastian Bach. Nielsen, "Bach had an inconceivable genius for music and a superhuman imagination. He moves with an admirable naturalness in the most complicated polyphony—and the outcome is always pure music. In the beginning of the great Fantasia and Triple Fugue in E flat major—isn't it as if the gates are thrown open to the radiant universe?" We were about to take leave, but now Nielsen had warmed to his subject, "Listen, I think Maren (the family's faithful housekeeper) has prepared a little refreshment; won't you come up with me?" There was a roast chicken and a glass of beer. We lit our cigars. "Let's play a duet on the piano; how about Mozart's symphony in E flat major, I like

10

that so much." It turned out the drollest piano duet in my experience, for it was played with incessant interruptions and comments. In order not to overstep the bounds of truth I won't state what he might possibly have said—after all it is a long time ago—but one phrase has stuck in my mind, "Mozart moves with the unerring steps of a somnambulist". At length we got through the first movement, and stopped there. A piano duet with Carl Nielsen had for me become a gratis lesson in advanced composition.

On another occasion I asked him how he felt when he wrote "Maskarade". "Those days stand out in my memory; I'll express it in this way: my own ego dwindled to something quite tiny, and I felt like a tube through which there flowed a stream, and I wrote with great ease; in that way Act Two was finished in twenty-odd days." Only many years later—once I spoke to him on the phone— I asked him again about "Maskarade"; how on earth he got the idea for the sublime passage in Act Three where the masks are discarded. "Well, don't you know the feeling that may seize you the day after you've been to a grand party—a feeling of wistfulness, transience."

Much has been said about the perfect first act, dramatically and musically— and it is certainly true—but it should not be forgotten that some of the best music is to be found in the last act of the opera—the cocks' dance, the priceless mime, and the above-mentioned scene of unmasking.

On our walks together we did not only talk about music. Self-taught, Nielsen was extraordinarily well read in world literature. The ancient Greeks were his special favourites. "I advise you to get acquainted with Greek pottery." He was interested in Plato to the end of his life. "The Republic" was at his bedside when he died.

After two years our night walks came to an end, for in June 1914 Nielsen resigned from the post as Conductor Royal after six years of office. Nielsen had always been on good terms with his orchestra. He had never regarded, let alone treated his subordinates as "slaves"—a not uncommon attitude among persons raised those few feet above the orchestra. He was far too human for that sort of thing, and being an ex-member of the orchestra he knew where the shoe might pinch. There was yet another side to the matter: each single musician was aware that he had to do with a creative artist of genius. This respect and reverence among my old colleagues for the extraordinary I have always kept as a beautiful memory.

I have sometimes wondered whether Nielsen left many, perhaps great works unwritten by spending six years of his valuable time as an executant musician. The question is irrelevant I suppose, since we do not know Nielsen's inmost motives. He loved conducting—and was quite right in doing so. It should also be borne in mind that all his life, from his childhood and early youth, he had ranked with the common musicians. I think that it must have been an incentive for him to remain in contact with the practical work in the orchestra. So the question is really whether he could have done without this incentive. It is, however, highly surprising that, during these six years when his head was full of other composers' music, he should possess mental vigour and bodily strength for creative work of his own.

Nielsen did not give up practical work entirely when he resigned from the theatre. In 1915 he was appointed teacher of musical theory and composition at The Royal Academy of Music, and at the same time he became a member of the board of directors. Furthermore, he was given the post as conductor in The Musical Society. Compared with the strenuous years at the theatre these tasks were of a more peaceful nature, and they left him far more time for his proper calling. In June he moved out of his old home, as he was offered an honorary residence at Frederiksholms Kanal 28 A. He lived here with his family till his death in 1931.

Nielsen had presumably been planning a new symphony for some length of time, even before he left the theatre—the magnificent "The Inextinguishable". One morning about the time when he was working on the fourth symphony, I came across him during a stroll on the Christianshavn Ramparts. Naturally I asked him what he was working on. "A new symphony, in fact. I have got an idea about a duel between two kettledrums, something about the war. I've also a subsidiary theme in the first movement, it runs in parallel thirds for some time. It is not quite like me, but it came out in that way, so it's going to be like that all the same."

The symphony left Nielsen's forge on the 14th of January 1916, having been in the crucible for about six months, and shortly after, on the first of February, the original performance took place. I had taken part in all the rehearsals and witnessed the first performance of "The Inextinguishable". What glorious days! The audience's tumultuous ovations after the symphony left no doubt that Nielsen with this music had touched the basic feelings in the inmost recesses of the human soul and released these feelings in his overwhelming and powerful musical language. Great as the victory had been which Nielsen had won with his "Espansiva", this was his decisive triumph. After this gigantic battle his opponents lay felled. Everyone admitted his genius; here was the key to the understanding of Nielsen's music—all his preceding works, too.

In between the last two great symphonies a rich crop was harvested in other fields, too: the Violin Concerto, op. 33, the Sonata for Violin and Piano, No 2, op. 35, the charming, humorous Serenata in vano, and together with Thomas Laub "A Score of Danish Songs", collection I (1915). Each of them wrote the tunes for one half of the texts; and a second collection appeared already in 1917. Nielsen's share was great art on a small scale, and his musical genius has left us a treasure of richly faceted music in these simple songs and airs.

The Violin Sonata No 2 stands apart in my memory. One evening towards the end of August 1912 I was invited to Nielsen's house together with the pianists Henrik Knudsen and Christian Christiansen. We were going to hear the new work. Nielsen took out his violin, and Knudsen sat down at the piano. The first

12

impression was almost too strong: the abundance of ideas, the abrupt transitions, and the rapidly changing moods—wildness and lyricism. The vigour and greatness of the music was clear to us, and we understood that something new had been created here in a quite unprecedented manner. And how expressively Nielsen played the moving Adagio of the Sonata on his violin.

Nielsen was not a brilliant violinist, but his intonation was perfectly correct; his tone, though not very full, was clear and steady, and his rhythm and phrasing bore the mark of a great musician. Nielsen was also an amusing partner in a string quartet. When he was in the mood for fun, he might take it into his head to play small tricks with fairly unimportant passages in his part—by a slight, scarcely noticeable exaggeration. Nielsen had always an exquisite sense of humour —indeed, on a much larger scale, he was Holberg's equal.

By now Carl Nielsen had grown a central figure in the musical life of his day, and great honours were heaped upon him. This position, however, entailed a hampering of his creative work by irrelevant things: people kept pestering him to get letters of recommendation, he was disturbed on the telephone etc. Already at this time Carl had found sanctuaries with various friends whose doors were always open to him: with Miss de Thygeson at Damgaard near Fredericia, with Vera and Carl Johan Michaelsen at Humlebæk, with the Mannheimers in Gothenburg, and in his own summer residence at Skagen. A considerable part of his time was spent on travels and on conducting his own works. The Swedes in particular took Nielsen and his music to their hearts, whereas he was variously appreciated in the countries south of Denmark, so that he unfortunately did not live to see the international recognition of his music—Scandinavia excepted.

The following years until Nielsen's death added a rich store of great and peculiar works, and each new opus was a milestone in his struggle towards tonal and formal mastery and independence. This perpetual process resembles the course of Beethoven's life. 1916 was the year of the great piano compositions: the Chaconne, op. 32, and Theme with Variations, op. 40. While he was busy with these variations, I met him one day in a tramcar. "I have found a theme which is to form the basis of a number of variations for the piano. It is a rather peculiar theme, beginning in B minor and ending in G minor. All the same—it had to develop like that." The audience, however, do not notice anything, since Nielsen has switched imperceptibly, as if by magic, into B minor at the beginning of the first variation. Nielsen enriched our stock of piano music with two other extensive works: the Suite, op. 45, from 1919, and Three Piano Pieces, op. 59 (posthumously) from 1928. Other major works from this period of growth are: "Pan and Syrinx", op. 49 (1918), the music for "Aladdin", the music for "The Mother" (1920) and "Springtime in Funen", op. 42, (1921). This last work was written at the time when the composition of the majestic Fifth Symphony was in progress. I quote a letter to Christian Christiansen, dealing with "Springtime in Funen", in which Nielsen displays the lightheartedness so characteristic of the inhabitants of his native Funen: "Damgaard, Fredericia. 27.8.21. Dear Christiansen, Thank you for lending me the book; I have kept it far too long. And thanks for your greetings from Ubberup! How I should love to be together with the three of you. —But I have been working hard, and in between the work on the symphony I've finished a Lyric Humoresque for soli, chorus, and orchestra. It's something I had taken on several years ago. The text is by Aage Berntsen. It has become quite a big affair (30 to 40 pages)—and I've amused myself by trying to give it a flavour of Funen humour and "feeling". It's going to be performed in Odense next year, and I hope that God and Mr Høeberg will give it their blessing. How is life with you? What have you been doing? You might write me a letter; you know what feelings I cherish about you. Give my regards to Thorvald Nielsen, if you see him; he has a share in the same feelings. Your affectionate friend, Carl Nielsen."

After Nielsen had got "Springtime in Funen" off his hands he was able to concentrate on the Fifth Symphony. The work on the second movement in particular was done at a furious prestissimo—but he had to pay dearly for this burst of energy. He suffered his first serious attack of angina pectoris in the spring of 1922. Here is an excerpt from my diary: 10.10.22. Some days ago I spent a pleasant hour at Carl Nielsen's home. I came round in the morning to deliver some press criticisms from the previous summer at Salzburg. Christian Christiansen and I had played his second Violin Sonata at the summer festival. He was standing in the corridor and invited me in to tea. We talked about his illness; he has had serious heart trouble for some time, caused by far too strenuous work on his compositions. Told me that while he worked on the last movement of the Fifth Symphony he had several times carried on from ten in the morning till five the next morning without feeling any apparent fatigue. But after some months came the reaction. He is feeling better now, though.

The night before this entry had seen the first performance of the fine Wind Quintet composed immediately after the completion of the Fifth Symphony. But how strange: Here is no trace of flagging inspiration. This holds true of everything that followed until he laid down his pen for good. In this respect Nielsen shared the fate of his two great predecessors Mozart and Beethoven, whose creative powers were never impaired by the pressure of external circumstances.

Yet another gift to the Danish people was the publication of the Song Book for the Folk High Schools, to which Nielsen had contributed some fifty tunes. In 1923 our violin repertory was enriched by the monumental Prelude and Theme with Variations for Violin Solo, op. 48, and as late as in 1928 the daring, modernistic Preludio e Presto for Violin Solo, op. 52. In 1924 a great part of his time was taken up by arranging music for and editing the song book "Denmark".

The ninth of June 1925 was a memorable day, the great master's 60th birthday. Few or none of Denmark's great sons have been celebrated in such a grandiose manner—except Hans Christian Andersen, perhaps. The King made him a Knight Commander of the Order of the Danebrog, and all day long presents and greetings kept pouring in from far and near. The festivities reached their climax with the

Corporal Nielsen (abt. 1882).

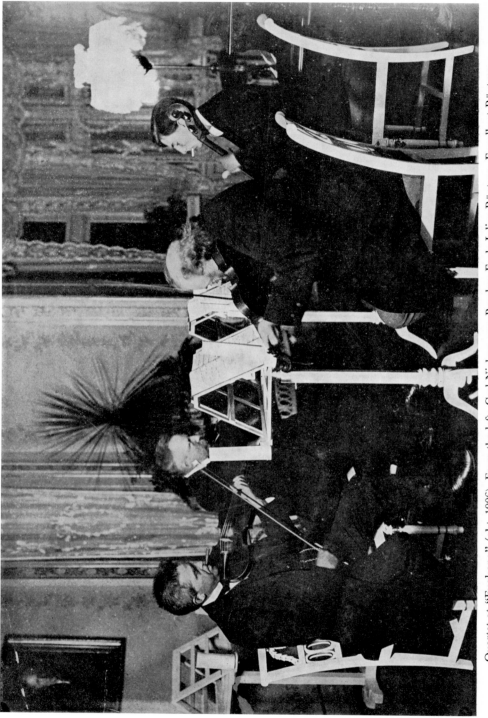

Quartet at "Fuglsang" (abt. 1906). From the left: Carl Nielsen, van Brucken-Fock, Julius Röntgen, Engelbert Röntgen.

gala concert in the Tivoli in the evening and the subsequent banquet at Nimb's. The first part of the programme opened with the Suite for Strings, op. 1, which had had its original performance in this same place. After this Peder Møller played the Violin Concerto. The second part, conducted by himself, consisted of the Fifth Symphony and "Springtime in Funen". Under endless applause he was presented with two big laurel wreaths after the concert. Afterwards some 350 persons assembled for a banquet at Nimb's. When Nielsen entered—accompanied by his wife, Anne Marie Carl Nielsen, his daughters Irmelin Eggert Møller and Anne Marie Telmanyi, his son Hans Børge and Maren—he was received with enthusiastic applause to the strains of the march from "Aladdin".

This is not the place to report the many speeches made by prominent personalities in Danish cultural life. But the master's own words in his reply deserve mentioning (quoted from my diary): Carl Nielsen described his childhood in outline "—brought up as I was in worldly and spiritual poverty—this last epithet does not refer to my parents, for they were—this goes without saying, really—always just as they should be (laughter). My mother always said to me: 'You should always endeavour to carry out your work to the best of your ability, and don't forget that Hans Christian Andersen was poor like you.' These words of my mother's I have always borne in mind. When I am honoured in this way to-day, I must protest that this is far too much (No! No!) Yes, ladies and gentlemen, it is too much; I cannot agree with you. For what I have done, I have done with delight, it has been a labour of love. Many others might have done what I have done, it is just that I have been lucky enough to have time and favourable circumstances for my work. When I have been working I have never, in fact, said to myself that this or that work of mine was going to be so great and outstanding as you tell me it is, I have just tried to carry out my work to the best of my ability in each single case". This was in brief what Nielsen said in his reply.

In the middle of the banquet came the sound of brass music, and a torchlight procession was approaching. We had to leave the supper. Nielsen stepped out on the open terrace. Thousands of people had turned up, and a wave of heartfelt gratitude and warmth surged up towards the artist. When Nielsen appeared, he was greeted with enthusiasm. After the singer Poul Wiedemann's beautiful words Nielsen began to speak. "I thank you all for your torches, which bring warmth and light. I take them to express that, in your opinion, I have something of this in me. I do not know it myself. But I tell you that there are many, many talents in this country that are not given a chance to develop. All of you have some of these faculties in you. And now I want to tell you that I have never composed anything so beautiful as what I have seen here to-night. Should I ever be able to express in music what this is, then listen to me. My dear friends! We are all made of the same stuff, all of us have life's faculties in us, if only we would use these faculties. I myself am so very little, and it is by chance that I became the man that I am. But let us together give three cheers for music, for all the light that shines in Denmark." It was half past two before we broke up, and the grand old man could go home and rest on his laurels.

With all these honours, expressive of a whole nation's gratitude, in mind, I was much surprised to find him in a very pessimistic mood during a short walk from his home to the Royal Exhange shortly after. He spoke about his youth and all his hardships. "Oh yes, now they praise me, but it doesn't matter now that I can do whatever I like; but the many years in my youth when it might have been a help for me, when—never mind . . ." Nielsen dismissed the thought with a gesture of his hand.

In the autumn of 1925 Nielsen was to surprise us once more; the completion of a new great achievement was drawing near—the Sixth Symphony. Like so many times before the new work was finished in the last moment before the planned first performance. (Diary 17.11.25): As part of the festivities on the occasion of Carl Nielsen's 60th birthday the Royal Theatre gave a performance of "Maskarade" to-night with himself as conductor. The performance was lively, and after prolonged plaudits at the end of the last act he appeared on the platform to thank the audience for the enthusiastic applause. Carl Nielsen called me this afternoon, asking me to give a message to a man whom he would refer to me as he had to isolate himself now and did not want to be disturbed by telephone calls. The reason was that he had not yet finished the last movement of the new symphony which the Royal Theatre Orchestra are going to perform on the 11th of December. I don't remember who that gentleman was.

After the first performance the audience were somewhat bewildered, and the press criticisms ranged from eulogy to the opposite. The Sixth Symphony has often been eclipsed by Nielsen's other great symphonies. Quite unjustly. Seen at a distance this work does in fact represent the height of Nielsen's masterly command of polyphony. All through he operates with purely thematic material. There is, indeed, some gaiety, but this gaiety moves on a higher plane, and the undercurrent has often a touch of something demoniacal, which momentarily lapses into downright eeriness. Nielsen himself told me that Variation IX is Death knocking at the gate. With this knowledge in mind it is not difficult to interpret what each instrument represents: The big drum the knocking; the xylophone bony Death; the deep tuba the black void. Nielsen explained on, "But I want to defy death—and then follows the flourish". Variation IX may also be taken as a burlesque joke—as indeed has been done—this only goes to show how ambiguous great art may be. Another uncanny passage is the trombones' brutal interruption in the middle of the waltz (Var. VI); the *joie de vivre* being crushed by evil powers. It is smouldering already at the beginning of the waltz with the discordant basses. The magic spell of the Humoresque is elicited by an exquisite use of all the artistic effects of contemporary music: polytonality and a polyrhythmical pattern; but employed for a definite artistic purpose with the restraint of the master mind. Egisto Tango, the Conductor Royal, once said, "The

Sixth Symphony by Carl Nielsen is a perfect masterpiece written by a perfect master." It ought to be played more frequently.

The strain of his heart trouble made our conversations take a turn to subjects we had not touched upon before. (Diary 1.6.27): Lunch with Carl Nielsen. At table we spoke about Stravinsky's "The Soldier's Tale", which has just been performed at The New Theatre. Carl Nielsen said, "The human body is equally unattractive to me when it is too fat and when the skeleton is too clearly visible." In his opinion Stravinsky belonged to the last category. Among many other subjects we discussed death and the eternal life, and Carl Nielsen remarked, "I dismiss the idea of an eternal life, and don't know if I really want to live for ever. I do not believe in supernatural things. Many things that look like miracles to us, are natural phenomena governed by laws we have failed to comprehend."

Of course there were also times when we spoke about our common ground of interest: art. (Diary 14.9.28): Carl Nielsen called me on the phone. We had a long talk about art occasioned by his latest work, a Concerto for clarinet and orchestra, which we have rehearsed these last few days, and which is to be given a private performance to-night at Mr Michaelsen's home in Humlebæk. He told me that it had been criticized from certain quarters for lacking lyricism (which I do not think is true!) "My wife has also told me that I ought not be afraid of giving free play to my emotions, for I shall never overdo it, as I am not a sentimental nature. But lyricism carries with it the seeds of corruption. The great artists have had the power to detach themselves (and he mentioned Bach and Shakespeare in this connection). They have not, like the romantics, involved themselves personally in each note and each word they have written, for this would have broken them into a thousand bits; but their powerful intelligence has organized everything, created order out of chaos, and left a harmonious whole. But without endeavouring to be so, they are deeply personal. If a work of art really fascinates us, there must always be feeling behind it."

The mental energy manifested by the great works of his last years, forms an unaccountable contrast to his increasing bodily debilitation.

(Diary 21.9.31): With Carl Nielsen. He called me at seven and told me he was sitting by himself, and would I like to come and have a chat with him? Spoke about his illness. Is seized by small fits daily. Described his frame of mind by saying that he wanted to be below ground—such a depressing strain came over him. I told him that I feared death. So did he in his youth, but that fear passes off—he did not know it now. Like so many times before our talk turned to eternity and the possibility of a personal life after death. Carl Nielsen: "It is not impossible, you know, that there are spirits round us here, who may smile at us that we cannot understand these things. When we die it may be that senses are released which have been tied by our physical existence. What is a thought? Something entirely intangible, and yet the highest reality." Then we discussed Plato's doctrine of ideas. Apart from this he was pleased with the present rehearsals of "Maskarade" under the baton of the excellent Italian conductor

Egisto Tango. He had received a request from the Royal Library to present them with the manuscript of this opera. "I have been looking for it and found the rough draft of the score, written in pencil, together with some scraps of paper, but that was what they wanted most of all—they are curious chaps, these library people." Later on Mrs Carl Nielsen came home. Ate; but Carl Nielsen just an apple. "For I want to be slim now." Played a rubber of bridge with a young doctor whose name I've forgotten. Then Carl Nielsen and I withdrew to his study. He took out the piano arrangement of "Maskarade". "There's something I want to ask you. Don't you think we can let Jonna Neiiendam sing this passage an octave below, and make it a little easier for her—I should like her very much to sing this part—I think she is so good".

As we were standing there together at the grand piano, I was suddenly moved by the thought that this was probably our last meeting. I managed to say, a little awkwardly perhaps, "I like your music so much." He did not say anything, did hardly smile I think, but put his arm round me and looked into my eyes with his strangely fervent look—the same radiant eyes that I remembered from our first meeting.

Some days before Nielsen was sent to the hospital for the last time, I caught a glimpse of him at a distance; he was standing on the esplanade outside the door of the Royal Theatre with his hat pulled down over his eyes.

Carl Nielsen died on the night of the 3rd October.

The most detailed biography is found in Torben Meyer's and Frede Schandorf Petersen's "Carl Nielsen. Kunstneren og Mennesket" I—II (København, 1947—48). This book has not been translated, but Torben Meyer has written a summary in English for Robert Simpson's "Carl Nielsen, Symphonist" (London, 1952). Supplementary biographical material is found in Carl Nielsen's "My Childhood" (London, 1953) and in Johannes Fabricius' "Carl Nielsen. En billedbiografi. A Pictorial Biography" (in Danish and English. København, 1965). Carl Nielsen's collection of essays "Levende Musik", which contains valuable information about his artistic views, is also available in an English translation: "Living Music" (London, 1953).

(Translated by N. Bugge Hansen)

ORCHESTRAL WORKS AND CHAMBER MUSIC

by

POVL HAMBURGER

Carl Nielsen's output included almost all musical genres from simple popular songs and five-note piano pieces to large-scale forms as opera and symphonies, and in all fields he produced works of high artistic quality, carrying the stamp of his strong, deeply original creative power. But he reached his highest attainments as a symphonist, and it was mainly in that capacity he attracted attention abroad. The six symphonies that came into existence between 1892 and 1925 thus stand out as the true milestones in his work, clearly marking the way his development led him: from a predominantly Scandinavian late classicism to a rather advanced international modernism.

Next to the symphony chamber music was the instrumental form which had the greatest attraction for Nielsen throughout life but especially during his youth and early maturity; naturally enough, considering his evidently innate sense of clear and concise form combined with exceptional gifts for counterpoint. His first attempts as a composer were accordingly within the field of chamber music. Dating from the years 1881—1887 are a number of student works, which remain unpublished, including a string quartet in F major, semi-publicly performed in 1888 without receiving any press criticism. The first works actually to count in so far as they were subjected to public critique and subsequently published, were both finished in 1888: a string quartet in G minor, later revised and issued in 1900 as op. 13, and a string quintet in G major, posthumously published in 1937 in Edition Dania. Both works are still mainly traditional in form as well as in manner, the influence of Johan Svendsen being particularly prominent, but in many places individual touches and progressive traits are noticeable. This is especially true of the quartet which, although it cannot be regarded as a preliminary study for the first symphony in the same key, completed four years later, nevertheless includes some phrases that occur again almost unaltered in the symphony.

With the *Little Suite for Strings in A minor* Nielsen takes the first step from chamber music to orchestral works. The composition was written in the same year (1888) as the quartet and the quintet but no doubt completed later than those works in spite of its being numbered op. 1. Form and expression are still

19

by and large influenced by Nordic-romantic tradition, but all the same Nielsen's own artistic physiognomy is already clearly discernible, and at the same time it becomes apparent how thoroughly he had trained himself by the writing of the preceding chamber works. This is felt both in the solid, almost impeccable part writing and in the clear and sure treatment of form. Combined with the lively, thoroughly inspiratory flow of the music this has brought about that in spite of the almost eighty years behind it the suite may still be heard with un-adulterated pleasure.

The suite has three movements: I. *Prelude. Andante con moto,* A minor, C. II. *Intermezzo. Allegro moderato,* D minor, 3/4 (with trio part in A major and coda in D major). III. *Finale. Andante con moto,* A minor, C.—*Allegro con brio,* A major, C.

A point of formal technique worthy of special mention is the effective way in which Nielsen connects the first and last movements by common thematic material, thus forming a circle of the whole work. The elegiac theme which opens the prelude:

Ex. 1

also forms the basis of the slow introduction to the *allegro* of the finale. Nor is that all. In the *allegro* movement, constructed on the sonata principle, it turns up again at the climax of the development—at first faintly and fragmentarily, then in its entirety and in full glory on the violins. After that the final phrase splits off (b), and a succession of dogged repetitions—eventually alternating between violins and basses—leads directly into the restatement where the figure is retained, moreover, as an *ostinato* counterpoint to the main theme as a whole. Then it disappears, only to emerge again for the last time as bass in the final cadence, thus taking its leave with a short, pithy farewell.

As employed by Carl Nielsen in this case, the so-called 'cyclic' principle is not only of formal importance but is directly bound up with the inner meaning of the work—viz. that the opening theme by breaking through in the finale appears as the leading idea of the whole. The incentive to this procedure Nielsen probably received from abroad—through Liszt, César Franck a. o.—but the manner in which he turns it to account is felt to be original and to promise things to come within his own production. The cyclic form is indeed found again twenty-five years later in the fourth symphony, 'The Inextinguishable', but now with a deeper spiritual background and developed in a more grandiose manner.

Although the suite in A minor is no truly symphonic work, being written for strings only, its overall character contains many elements clearly indicating the future symphonist, and so it is perhaps not wholly unwarranted to regard this work as the true 'prelude' to Nielsen's achievements as a symphonist. At any rate, by its intrinsic qualities it merits such a designation more than does his first attempt at writing for a symphonic orchestra, an attempt dating from the very next year, 1889.

The manuscript of this work, which is scored for the 'big' orchestra of the time (the brass group consisting of 4 horns, 2 trumpets and 3 trombones) is headed 'Symphony'. Presumably, then, Nielsen intended to compose an entire symphony, but only an *allegro* movement in F major was actually completed. Like the two preceding chamber works and the suite for strings the movement contains not a few traits indicative of future achievements, but the work, constructed on the traditional sonata principle, suffers particularly under the diffuseness of the development section, which is out of all proportion to the weight of the material. Nielsen was not satisfied with the result himself, and the movement has remained unpublished. Under the not very appropriate title: *Symphonic Rhapsody* it is occasionally performed, however.

In the following year, 1890, Nielsen returns to chamber music with the *String Quartet in F minor*. Published in 1892 as op. 5 this work is in several respects a milestone in Nielsen's career as a composer. To be true, the style is still influenced by that of his predecessors, especially Svendsen, and to no small extent by that of Brahms. But if this quartet is compared with that in G minor, written only two years before, it is easy to see that it marks an important step towards a clarification of his individuality as an artist. The themes have acquired a greater pithiness, and the somewhat loose texture—in the G minor quartet particularly noticeable in the first and last movements—has now given place to a more organic, tension-filled development of the material. These traits at once become apparent in the first movement with its impetuous main theme:

Ex. 2

The second movement, *Un poco adagio*, has for its main theme a warmly singing melody, marked by Carl Nielsen's already strong partiality for persistent repetition of the minor third, and in the ensuing *Allegretto scherzando* he reveals his characteristic sense of genuine humour in the interplay between the four instruments—now light and humorous, now bluffly burlesque. But now the young composer had relieved himself of almost all that he had on his mind in writing this quartet. In spite of an honest attempt to vie with the first movement as regards a display of energy, the finale is of a more superficial and thus a less interesting character.

At its first performance in April 1892 the quartet was enthusiastically received by the audience as well as by the critics, and its success was confirmed at a concert given by the composer himself a few weeks later. During the following years it was heard far and wide, not only in Europe but also in America, and it was thus the first work by Nielsen to become internationally well-known. It is said that when in Berlin in 1894 the young Danish composer was introduced to the great Belgian violinist Eugene Ysaye, the latter demonstrated his previous knowledge of Carl Nielsen simply by whistling the opening bars of the main theme of the F minor quartet!

Even in his early youth Nielsen had cherished the hope that he might one day "make big music", and what he had in mind was probably first and foremost the orchestra, the symphony. The above F major *allegro* from 1889 constitutes the first, embryonic attempt at a realization of this hope. The fulfilment took place with *Symphony No. 1 in G minor*, begun in 1891 and completed during the following year.

The very nature of this work, Nielsen's first 'great' one, means fulfilment and promise at the same time. It marks the end of his youthful struggle to realize himself, his individuality, surrounded by a very old, but still apparently paramount tradition; but at the same time it heralds his years of maturity when, from the newly won territory, he was to go on, step by step, breaking new ground within the world of his art. It is thus significant that even at an advanced age Nielsen did not look back upon his first symphony as merely a 'juvenile work', but continued to acknowledge it as a valid expression of his thoughts, feelings and intentions as a creative artist, even at that time.

But what were Nielsen's intentions as an artist? What was his personal attitude towards the music, past and contemporary, that rushed to meet him from the moment when he began his work as an artist?

In the section on Danish music in Adler's *Handbuch der Musikgeschichte* Knud Jeppesen gives a brief evaluation of Nielsen as a creative musician. Having stressed the remarkably "atavistic" quality of Nielsen's artistic appearance, he goes on to explain: ". . . with the fresh and uncorrupted senses of primitive man he contemplates his material, undisturbed by every tradition, just as if he were the very first man to see it, and through him it acquires a new, hitherto undreamt-of quality of expression." No doubt this touches on something quite essential, but the words must be understood in the right way. "Undisturbed by every tradition" must of course not be taken to mean independent of every tradition. On the contrary the origin of Nielsen's art was not only intimately bound up with the immediate past, but—at least that became the case in the course of time—it also traced still farther back, as regards certain elements even back to Gregorian chant. What was new, or rather: renewing, was indeed due, as Jeppesen puts it, to the *way* in which he contemplated the material—"as if he were the first man to see it". Thus Nielsen was neither a classicist nor a modernist, neither a reactionary nor an avant-gardist; he had certain features derived from all, but he was and remained—himself.

Therefore, when writers so often emphasize that from the very beginning Nielsen was in opposition to contemporary musical trends, actually declining to accept his inheritance with the assets and liabilities, this must of necessity be understood with qualifications. Another thing is that being a creative artist with a natural desire for self-assertion he had to seek beyond a *status quo* and

22

consequently to react against certain phenomena within the established order. The question is, then, in what respects he did react and from what inner motives.

In order to come to grips with this we must bear in mind the special problem, always topical in the field of aesthetics: the relative importance of what is popularly called 'feeling' and 'thought', more scholarly: the subjective and the objective. As to that, Carl Nielsen has of course given his opinion himself—e.g. and in particular in his charming collection of essays, "Living Music", from 1925—and in a way of which we may do well to take cognizance, because his own works of art clearly demonstrate that he did not preach one doctrine while following another himself. What he disliked from the very first was just the rampant subjectivism in art, too strong an emphasis on the purely emotional without the necessary control by the rational. In music this had resulted in an excessive exploitation of the harmonic element to the detriment of rhythm and melody, and as regards melody it had led to a weakening of the sense of the innate qualities of interval. It is in connection with some critical comments on the morbid and 'überschwängliche' in Wagner's music, in Carl Nielsen's opinion, that he makes the declaration of love of the good interval which has since become almost proverbial:

"Against this style of music there is, then, no other remedy than the cultivation of the first basic intervals. We must demonstrate to the surfeited that a melodic third should be regarded as a divine gift, a fourth as an experience, and a fifth as the greatest joy. Thoughtless greed undermines health. We see, then, that it is essential to maintain the connection with the primitive."

Thus Nielsen's repudiation of the excessively subjective in late-romantic music is balanced by a correspondingly higher appreciation of the objective element, the intellectual control during the process of composition. This attitude was bound to find expression in attempts at a renovation of those very elements that seemed to him to constitute the primordial elements of music: melody and rhythm, which in its turn almost as a matter of course resulted in a rebirth of the linear principle.

Like the earlier works even the first symphony follows classical examples in so far as it is written in four distinct movements with the usual tempo scheme: *allegro, andante, allegro, allegro*; the same holds true of the choice of keys for the individual movements: G minor, G major, E flat major and G minor, respectively; that is, in a way, nothing more radical than may still be met with in Brahms. But as regards the material itself, its nature and treatment, the public was confronted by something hitherto unheard-of in Danish music. The symphony was in G minor, but nonetheless it began with a C major chord and, moreover, ended in a quite strongly supported C major. And what have those two keys to do with each other at all? Apparently not much, at least if the matter is regarded from a traditional major-minor point of view. The frequent occurrence of a minor seventh (B flat) in C major as well as of a major sixth (E) in G minor gives the two keys a not quite negligible touch of modality, however, thus establishing a tonal relationship between them, not present in 'classical' C major and G minor. Moreover, a struggle between the two tonalities goes on throughout the work, reaching its final settlement in the definite establishment of the C tonality. Nielsen has now taken the first step towards the application of the principle called 'progressive tonality' by Robert Simpson, the English composer and scholar, in his book on Carl Nielsen as symphonist, a principle which was to become a leading one within his symphonic writing.

The *first movement* is marked *Allegro orgoglioso* ('proud', 'haughty') in perfect agreement with its proud and stern character and anything but effeminate harmonies. After the notorious opening chord of C major the main theme is announced in a harsh G minor:

Ex. 3

Already typically 'Nielsenesque' by its insistent rhythm and 'close' intervals this is as it were a concentrate of the essential character of the whole movement. The motive is repeated a fifth higher, and now the first group, twenty bars in length, expands in a freely formed bold curve, ending with a *crescendo* in a short, firm G minor cadence. After a connecting passage comes the second subject, entering surprisingly in D flat major (so distant from G minor) but gradually modulating to B flat major, the classically 'correct' relative key. The gentler, lyrical nature of this section forms an effective contrast to what went before, but the material of the main theme returns in the epilogue, and after a forceful *crescendo* it brings the exposition to a conclusion in a *tutti ff*. The development section, which treats material drawn from the themes already put forward, is written with an imaginativeness astonishing in so young a symphonist, combined with a no less astonishing technical mastery. Through three phases of increasing length and intensity the music is brought to a purposeful climax of immense rhythmic tension leading directly into the recapitulation. The coda begins *piano pianissimo* with a *fugato* based on the main theme in augmentation, and gradually builds up a tremendous dynamic rise culminating in a furious *stretto* which concludes the movement with a last firm statement of the main theme in an abrupt cadence.

After this violent outburst, particularly effective because the whole movement is characterized by a terseness almost reminding us of the first movement of Beethoven's fifth symphony, the *second movement, Andante,* produces a well-calculated relaxation. Its ternary form with broadly planned, tonally contrasting middle section and the dynamically heightened repetition of the main section shows the influence of corresponding movements in Brahms's symphonies, especially in No. 1, but the overall character is entirely Nielsen's own. Beginning with the dreamy, elegiac main theme the whole movement flows on in a single uninterrupted breath, deeply moving owing to its Nordic-lyric substance and at the same time calling forth admiration by the organic development of the material.

The *third movement* has the nature of a *scherzo* as regards its motives as well as the tempo (*Allegro comodo*) and the 6/4 time; but the form is individually treated and has features derived from both sonata-form and rondo. Typical of Nielsen is especially the brilliant main theme consisting of two four-bar motives, the first characterized by syncopation and an obstinate twisting within the range of a major third, the second by vivaciously conflicting intervals due to the characteristic alternation between major and minor thirds:

Ex. 4

Contrasting with this theme are the more solemn *cantabile* second theme and the martial epilogue group, the violently complicated rhythm of which momentarily recalls the first movement.

The *finale* (*Allegro con fuoco*) is borne along by a continuous drive similar to that of the first *allegro*, but preserving the classical qualities of a finale by a generally more relaxed course. The whole is like one single springy march, a character manifested at once in the distinct, boldly developed main theme:

Ex. 5

Like the first movement even this is introduced by a vigorous C major chord, and in the following the above-mentioned 'struggle' between C major and G minor comes to a head until finally C major carries the day in the concluding grandiose plagal cadence.

The first performance of the symphony at a concert with the Orchestra of the Royal Theatre on 14th March 1894, conducted by Johan Svendsen, was enthusiastically received by the audience, and even the critics were on the whole highly appreciative. Already during the next years the work was performed several times abroad, particularly in Sweden and Germany, attracting great attention even there.

With his first symphony Nielsen had demonstrated to the full, both to his surroundings and to himself, the strong creative powers within him that gave grounds for expecting great things from his career as a composer. It is therefore natural that he should feel an urge to set to work immediately on new great tasks, involving the tackling of other genres. Thus appeared in the field of vocal music the lovely, classically inspired choral work 'Hymnus amoris' (1896) and the monumental first opera 'Saul og David' (1901).

In the field of chamber music too, Nielsen now entered a new domain. In

25

1895 he finished his first *Sonata for Violin and Piano in A major,* published the following year as op. 9. The combination of a solo instrument with piano had previously been put to use on a more modest scale in the two charming fantasy pieces for oboe and piano ('Romance' and 'Humoresque') of 1889. Here as well as in the songs op. 4 and op. 6 (1891) the piano mainly serves the function of an accompanying instrument; but in 1894 Nielsen wrote his first important key-board work, 'Symphonic Suite', op. 8, and in so doing he greatly enlarged his experience with regard to the capabilities of the piano as an independent instrument. An extensive employment of parallel octaves and of massive successions of chords in both hands—to which, by the way, he may have found incitement in Schumann, Brahms, César Franck a. o.—is, indeed, in evidence in the piano part of the sonata.

This work by the then thirty-year-old composer seems particularly suitable for a doing away with the myth of Nielsen as a pronounced 'anti-romantic'. The emotive, lyrical traits of his artistic being, prevailing throughout his life but, owing to his virile, healthy and sober nature, never degenerating into sentiment-ality or bombast, hardly ever manifested themselves more clearly than in this youthful work which from first to last seems conceived in an effortlessly happy inspiration. Still, it is anything but 'light' music. Particularly in the first two movements we find a multiplicity of motives, subtly treated, often on the basis of a counterpoint as ingenious as it is brilliant, and in addition harmony and modulation are treated with a freedom and daring that does not fall short of what had appeared so striking to the contemporary public already in the first symphony. The sonata had its first performance shortly after New Year 1896 and was published in the same year with a dedication to the great French violinist Henri Marteau. It did not arouse unqualified enthusiasm with the critics, but was thought to be too 'learned', too 'experimenting'.

The work has three movements: *Allegro glorioso—Andante—Allegro piacevole e giovanile.* The first and last movements are in A major, the middle movement in C sharp minor. The *first movement* begins with a springy, almost defiant theme:

Ex. 6

the nature of which is further emphasized by the speedy transfer of the motive from A major to F minor. Contrasting with this is the lyrically singing second subject. After a gently dreamlike beginning in C major the latter leads to a magnificent heightening of intensity, coming to a climax in a sparkling E major.

In the *second movement,* written in ternary form, the solemnly introspective, almost *religioso*-like mood of the first theme is shattered for a short while in the middle section by a light and cheerful episode, the naïve, almost folk-tune-like motive of which by a metamorphosis of genius gradually evolves from the heavily advancing subsidiary motive of the first theme:

Ex. 7

"One thing must grow out of another." Thus Carl Nielsen has himself characterized an aspect of the technique of composition particularly prominent in his own music. With regard to the gift for connecting even highly contrasting material by a transformation of motives so that the impression of an organic whole is preserved, scarcely any other modern composer comes closer to Beethoven than Nielsen.

With the finale the key of A major returns, and the character approaches that of the first movement, but without the agressiveness and tension-filled contrasts of the latter. In the uninterrupted adherence to the 3/4 time and the resilient syncopation, which at once characterize the main theme:

Ex. 8

we seem to find an as yet restrained precursor of what will be found more impressively developed in the first movement and the finale of the third and fourth symphonies respectively.

In 1898 Nielsen completed the *String Quartet in E flat major*, op. 14. Eight years had elapsed since he wrote the F minor quartet, and looking back upon the latter we find more than hints at the development that had taken place during the intervening time with regard to Nielsen's feeling for and mastery of the technique of quartet writing. This holds true especially of the *first movement, Allegro con brio,* where an air of grandeur is combined with a richly developed contrapuntal activity of all the parts within a firmly constructed form scheme. In the *second movement, Andante sostenuto*—strangely enough in the same key (E flat major) as the first—a brief diffident introduction is followed by the main theme:

Ex. 9

the broad lines and great expressivity of which seem to foreshadow the third movement of the second symphony, 'The Four Temperaments'. The *third movement, Allegretto pastorale,* has a main section reminiscent of the lighter Brahmsian scherzo:

Ex. 10

—a type for which Nielsen had a marked preference. The contrasting middle section is an eventually furiously worked-up presto in 6/8 time, after which the movement is concluded by a resumption of the *allegretto.* In the new work, as in the F minor quartet, Nielsen had his say in the first three movements. The vivacious *finale, Allegro coraggioso,* has a main theme with cutting fourths, closely related to the first theme of the finale of the first symphony.

Ex. 11

It seems a bit long-winded, however, measured by the intrinsic worth of the material.

In 1901, even before he had finished work on the opera 'Saul og David', Nielsen started on *Symphony No. 2,* an instance among many others of the great capacity for work which he preserved intact until in his last years ill-health checked it to some extent. While the first symphony like all the preceding instrumental works has no special title, Nielsen called his new symphony 'The Four Temperaments', having set himself the task in the four movements of the work to give a musical representation of the choleric, the phlegmatic, the melancholic and the sanguine temperaments respectively. He has related himself how he received the impulse to do so during a visit to a country inn in Zealand, where he saw hanging on the wall a coloured picture in four parts giving a naïve-symbolic representation of 'the temperaments'. "Here is the idea of a new symphony," his wife is reported to have said.

Must the symphony 'The Four Temperaments' then be regarded as 'programme music'? In a way, yes; in another way, no. On several occasions—in greatest detail in the chapter 'Words, Music and Programme Music' in his 'Living Music'—Nielsen has himself accounted for his opinion of this genre, its possibilities and limitations, thus furnishing us with the key to an understanding of his own way of interpreting his second symphony and how he wanted it to be interpreted. He writes e.g.: "When music, then, cannot possibly express concrete thoughts or acts and its relationship to words never can be anything but decoratively illustrating, it is much less able to express a whole, long, continuous programme." However, he does not wish wholly to reject the idea of a programme, provided the line is drawn properly between the fanciful and the possible. "If one limits oneself to a brief suggestion or title the music may illuminate and set off from many angles and in several ways . . . But the programme or the title must in itself contain a motive of feeling or movement, never one of thinking or concrete action."

The dividing line mentioned above is indeed never crossed in this symphony, the very nature of which allows it to be heard entirely as absolute music. Another thing is that on the face of it a subject like this does not strike one as particularly suitable for *symphonic* treatment, seeing that such a treatment does indeed presuppose not only a contrast between the individual movements, but also the establishing of more or less pronounced disparities within the single movement; at any rate that the material is seen in varying lights by a motivic-thematic process of development. This reservation is chiefly valid, however, if the contrast of character between the four temperaments is understood absolutely. With this subject in hand Baroque composers—such as the French *clavecinistes*—would no doubt have written a suite in four movements in which the choleric person would have behaved in a choleric way from start to finish—and the others in a correspondingly uniform manner. Modern times have developed a considerably deeper understanding of human mentality, however, they have opened our eyes to the fact that absolute characters just do not exist, but that the psychological mechanism as a whole is of a very complex nature. And as to Carl Nielsen, he had a highly developed understanding of human nature combined with a distinctly psychological perception. Faced with the problem presented to him by the new symphony he realized that 'the choleric person' is not exclusively choleric but that he knows of more quiet and relaxed moments, too; that the phlegmatic one *may* be roused to greater activity now and then—and correspondingly with regard to the other two. By virtue of this the second symphony is then what it professes to be—a truly symphonic work. Incidentally, it is no mere coincidence that this symphony is practically contemporaneous with the opera 'Saul og David', the musical strength of which is due especially to the monumental and at the same time subtle characterization of King Saul, whose nature seems recognizable in many ways in the first movement of the symphony.

If this symphony is compared with the first, written ten years before, the development gone through by the composer since then cannot be overlooked, of course, although the unsophisticated attractiveness characterizing the first great work of his youth will perhaps be missed to some extent. But his grasp of things has become firmer, the thematic material has acquired a higher degree of pithiness, and—not least—the rhythmic tension has been increased to a pronounced degree. Formally this symphony rests on the same—late classical—foundation as its predecessor, however: the first *allegro* is in sonata-form, both middle movements in ternary form, while the finale—exceptionally in Nielsen's symphonic works—is in rondo-form. But the sequence of keys is more free than had hitherto been the case in Nielsen's cyclic works: B minor—G major—E flat minor (!)—D major (with coda in A major).

The main themes of the four movements of the symphony—sufficient indications of their respective characters—are as follows:

Allegro collerico

Ex. 12

Allegro comodo e flemmatico

Ex. 13

Andante malincolico

Ex. 14

Allegro sanguineo

Ex. 15

Work on the symphony was finished in the late autumn of 1902, and the first performance took place as early as 1st December at a concert given by the "Danish Concert Society", incidentally only three days after the first night of 'Saul og David'. On both occasions Nielsen was himself the conductor.

During his stay in Athens the following year Nielsen wrote the *'Helios' Overture* in which, inspired by the clear sky of the South, he depicts the course of the sun, its rise, culmination and setting. In a way a fresh piece of programme music, but kept within the same limits as the symphony 'The Four Temperaments'. The new work is indeed written in an absolute-musical form, in this case an *allegro* movement in fairly regular sonata-form, surrounded by a slow introduction and conclusion. The only 'pointer' furnished by the composer is a short motto in four parts corresponding with the four main stages of the musical development: "Silence and darkness—then the sun rises with a joyous song of praise—it wanders its golden way—and sinks quietly into the sea."

(I). The opening *Andante tranquillo* is *pianissimo* with the deep strings in unison. Presently the four horns—over the double pedal C-G—state a motive with a peculiar dim colouring, determined by a repeated introduction of the 'primitive' seventh, B flat. (II). A crescendo to *forte* prepares a strong and broad, hymn-like melody:

Ex. 16

(III). Modulating to E major a blaring trumpet fanfare introduces the festal main theme of the *allegro*:

30

Ex. 17

(IV). After the climax (*forte fortissimo*) the *allegro* ebbs away in a *diminuendo* with a concomitant thinning out of sound, and returning to the *andante* tempo and the key of C major the movement is as it were extinguished in the deep C on the cellos in unison.

It is open to discussion whether the form chosen by Nielsen with its many contrasts, especially as regards tempo, was entirely serviceable to the description of nature that he had in view—whether, indeed, as maintained by Simpson, Nielsen had not been wiser to write a uniformly slow movement on the lines (but not in the style) of Wagner's 'Lohengrin' prelude. But apart from the fact that the magnificently drawn curve of the music: darkness-light-darkness, together with the orchestral and modulatory tension-slackening might seem graphic enough, the naturalistic element in the work ought hardly to be over-emphasized. No doubt Nielsen wanted primarily to reflect the *impression* left by this particular natural phenomenon on the mind of the spectator—from devout expectation through increasing fascination to quiet sadness—reminding us, in fact, of the classical cult of the sun. Virtually in close harmony with Beethoven's: "Mehr Ausdruck der Empfindung als Malerei". Interpreted in this way as to its intrinsic idea 'Helios' aligns completely with other works from the period in Nielsen's life which, hardly without reason, has been called his 'psychological' period: 'Saul og David', 'The Four Temperaments' and the choral work 'Sleep'.

The years 1905—06 were mostly devoted to the opera 'Maskarade', but Nielsen had time, after all, to compose a new chamber work, the *String Quartet in F major*. It is dated July 2nd 1906, only four months before 'Maskarade', and originally it had the title 'Piacevolezza' and the opus number 19. Revised later it was published in 1923 as op. 44.

With this work Nielsen's style as a writer of quartets reaches its final clarification. Although perhaps not quite so profound as the E flat minor quartet of ten years before it still surpasses its predecessor with regard to its purely technical qualities as chamber music. The texture is everywhere characterized by delicacy and transparency, and the four instruments are accorded equal treatment in a positively Haydnish manner, "like independent personalities engaging in brilliant conversation". In many ways the quartet shows traces of having been written at the same time as 'Maskarade'; Nielsen's genuine and kindly sense of humour, which achieves such great triumphs in the opera, has also left delicate and engaging impressions here. This is felt particularly in the last two movements—the *allegretto* with its alternately graceful and burlesque ideas, and the finale which in spite of its moderate *allegro-tempo* must be performed 'molto scherzando' and which owes its attraction especially to its gay and homely second subject. Weightiest are the first two movements—*Allegro non tanto e comodo* and the greatly expressive *Adagio con sentimento religioso* with its modally coloured main theme.

31

Owing to its tonal character the main theme of the first movement deserves special mention. Nielsen's penchant for a prompt flight from the main key—a fact intimately bound up with the intensive development of linear expansion—had already been in evidence in earlier works, but till then in such a way that the conclusion of the theme had been unambiguously tonal. The practice followed in the quartet by which the theme, beginning in F major, in the course of nine bars is carried through to a cadence a semitone higher (G flat major), thus marks in a way a further step in the direction of radicalism:

Ex. 18

Now it is of course easy to begin in one key and finish in another—any organist knows as much from his own use of modulation—what is peculiar to Nielsen is that the modulation is carried through not harmonically but purely melodically, so that the harmony of the other voices is directly determined by this fact. Surely Nielsen's unerring instinct—so often extolled—for the melodic interval, its qualities and possibilities, has rarely manifested itself more clearly than in this short but beautifully curving and flexible line, ending in a G flat major which is felt to be just as naturally relaxing and thus just as inevitable as if the goal attained had been the traditionally correct opening key.

During the next years the F major quartet was followed by other chamber works, partly of high quality, but Nielsen never returned to the writing of string quartets. Keeping in mind especially the two last quartets we may perhaps wonder why—and deplore the fact.

In 1908 Nielsen finished a new orchestral work: *Sagadrøm* ('The Dream of Gunnar'). He was inspired to write this while reading in 'Njal's Saga' the description of how Gunnar of Hlidarende in exile on his way to Norway goes to sleep, a sleep gradually developing into a horrible nightmare that finally fades away and vanishes. While neither 'Helios' nor 'The Four Temperaments' may rightly be classified as a tone-*poem,* 'Sagadrøm' belongs more obviously to this genre—a genre, incidentally, to which Nielsen did not feel greatly attracted and which he cultivated in only two later works: in the semi-impressionistic experiment 'Pan og Syrinx' (1918) and the occasional work: 'En Fantasirejse til Færøerne' ('An Imaginary Trip to the Faroe Islands') (1927).

In spite of its humble size—the playing time is only about ten minutes—'Sagadrøm' is remarkable for its extremely varying emotional contents. The piece cannot be classified in the same genre with 'Helios', and dynamically it does not rise to similar heights, but the disposition of material and instrumentation is in several ways analogous. This finds expression in the beginning and the close on the deep strings, in the exploitation of the brass, here in the form of a subdued 'chorale' on the trombones, with 'Nordic' colouring à la Hartmann, and in the employment of *fugato* in a greatly accelerated tempo. Preceding the final section

32

of the work, where a synthesis is formed of the principal melodic material, is an elaborate *cadenza* for woodwind, glockenspiel and strings, where each of the instruments involved is given free reins within the tempo indicated—a technique pointing forwards to the market-scene in the 'Aladdin'-music, written ten years later, where four orchestras play simultaneously, but now each in its own tempo.

Leaving 'Sagadrøm' out of account, the years 1907—09 to some extent mark a compositorial period of rest, during which Nielsen devoted his time chiefly to occasional works in the shape of music for plays and cantatas—most weighty among the latter is the 'Cantata for the Anniversary of Copenhagen University' (1908). But on the threshold of the year 1910 he experiences once again a tremendous intensification of his creative powers, the product of which is symphony No. 3, *'Sinfonia espansiva'*, op. 27.

Finished by the middle of 1911 and performed for the first time on 28th February 1912 at a concert with the Orchestra of the Royal Theatre arranged by Nielsen himself, the symphony marks, in its own field, the complete realization of his personal style, thus occupying a position in Nielsen's symphonic work similar to symphony No. 3, 'Eroica', in that of Beethoven. The composer said himself in an interview that with this new work he intended to protest against the soft smoothing out which he thought characterized so much Danish music up till then—"I want stronger rhythms, more advanced harmony."

Like the two preceding symphonies even No. 3 is in the classical four movements, the tempo of the first and last being *allegro,* and in the middle ones *andante* and a scherzo-like *allegretto,* respectively. The outlines of the traditional form types have also been preserved in the separate movements, although with marked individual traits determined by the material itself and by its treatment. The epithet, 'espansiva', has been transferred to the work as a whole from the first movement, 'Allegro espansivo'. 'Expansive' here alludes to the chiefly rhythmically conditioned expansive force and enormous growth in the development of motives and themes, especially in evidence in the first *allegro*. This moves continually in 3/4 time on a one-beat basis, confronting us with what Robert Simpson so aptly calls Nielsen's "athletic triple time", the same that controls the finale of the fourth and fifth symphonies and which is characterized by a rhythm at once firm and supple—very different from the often rigid, positively mechanical rhythm met with in much contemporary music, e.g. that of Stravinsky.

The "more advanced harmony" indicated by Nielsen himself shows itself notably in a harmonic bluffness, an almost unremittingly dissonant progress, in places even with polytonal features. As in the earlier works from the first symphony onward, a particular key is not maintained for long; in fact the music modulates incessantly, not at random, of course, but determined by the immense expansion of the melodic and rhythmic elements. The classic insistence on tonal unity within each single movement as well as the work as a whole had indeed been disregarded as early as in the second symphony, and in the third the liberalization in this respect has progressed a stage farther. Thus the first and last movements go from D minor to A major and from D major to A major respectively, the second movement from C major to E flat major; only the *allegretto* begins and ends in the same key, C sharp minor. The tonal goal of the whole symphony —cf. Simpson's 'progressive tonality'—is thus A major, finally reached with great cogency and brilliance.

The dominating part played by the rhythmic element in the symphony becomes clear from the very beginning—a vigorous *tutti* entry in unison on the note A, repeated through 14 bars in a rapid *accelerando* that builds up a violent tension, released at length by the main theme of the movement being, as it were, flung into space:

Ex. 19

The will to expand manifests itself at once in this brief motive, with intervals rising boldly towards the octave and with a concluding, resilient syncopation. Without any interruption of the flow the motive is carried on—first in free sequential treatment, then in rising and falling curves, gradually shifting from crotchets to quavers. Through more than a hundred bars this development goes on in two great waves, the last of which—that leads to the culmination—is set in motion by the main theme, too. At the tremendous *fff*-climax the motive appears for the third time—now on bassoons, trombones and tuba and in a key so distant from D minor as A flat minor—but immediately afterwards comes a *diminuendo* slackening, leading to the second group of the movement in A flat major:

Ex. 20

The lyrical, almost vegetating character, contrasting sharply with the preceding section, makes this subject a temporary point of rest, until the moving forces gather strength again and after a further climax bring the exposition to a close.

A more detailed analysis of the rest of the movement will not be attempted here. It must be emphasized, however, that in spite of the broad sweep of the movement, the often strongly brought-out periods of slackening and the no less strongly accentuated contrasts of motives, the whole course of the music is controlled by an unbreakable cohesive force, due partly to the rhythmic pulsation, incessant though varying in intensity, partly to the adherence to the basic motivic material of the main theme. Even the second subject, apparently of quite another character, is immediately related to the first subject by virtue of the concluding syncopation. An ingenious metamorphosis of this motive is carried out in the development. With a few bold strokes—the syncopation is left out and a triplet figure added—Nielsen creates a completely new physiognomy: the harshly concentrated manner disappears and is replaced by a waltz-like gliding—evidently a reminiscence, on a highly stylized level, of the fiddler's music of Nielsen's childhood in Funen:

Ex. 21

The recapitulation opens with the second group so that the material of the first group may be saved for the coda where it is combined with motives from the first group in a final heightening of tension, relieved in the glorious A major close of the movement.

The *second movement—Andante pastorale—*is rather in the character of a scenic idyll, thus forming an effective contrast to the first movement with its wide scope and nervous tension. The main section consists of a melody developed in calm curves by the strings in unison with no other accompaniment than a pedal C on the horns, later supplemented with the fifth, G, on the bassoons:

Ex. 22

This is a happy revelation of Nielsen's close affinity to pure monophony as it had reached its European highwater-mark in Gregorian chant, a connection that shows itself partly in the organic development of the melody, independent both of rhythmic symmetry and of a harmonic way of feeling, partly in the employment of the 'Mixolydian' minor seventh B flat.

An intermediary passage, in which two mutually contrasting episodes alternate several times, adds to the vigour and tension, but after a transition to the key of E flat major follows a recapitulation of the whole first subject. This passage is played by the entire orchestra, but the sound intensity is kept permanently subdued, and in this way the tone of sublime majesty is combined with a gentle warmth, which makes the passage one of the most delightful in the whole body of Carl Nielsen's work. A special colouring is obtained, moreover, by the combination of the melody with two human voices, a barytone and a soprano, that sing seemingly improvised coloraturas on the vowel "a".

The *third movement* has the character of a scherzo. As in earlier works there are, in the 2/4 time and the *allegretto* tempo, affinities to Brahms. The tone is one of unrefined merriment with many capricious ideas. Just as in the quartet in F major one is frequently reminded of the music of 'Maskarade', especially in the frolicsome second subject which is heard on the woodwind as a trio for oboes, and which calls the witty 'Cocks' Dance' in the opera to mind.

In a way the *finale* forms a worthy counterpart to the first *allegro* by its monumental grandeur and its richness and variety of life, besides corresponding,

3*

as we have seen, with the main tonal scheme of that movement. The character, however, is different. The somewhat rugged concentration that characterized great parts of the first movement has given way to a fresh, uncomplicated music in a regularly pulsating march-like rhythm which is started at once by the main subject, and which flows almost uninterruptedly through the whole movement.

Nielsen himself spoke about "the pulsating rhythm of work" in this connection:

Ex. 23

The healthy tuneful tone and the extended *Lied*-like presentation of this subject leaves an impression of conformity with older finale subjects like that of Brahms's first symphony or the "Freude" subject of Beethoven's 'Ninth', but at the same time it has something of the tone of Carl Nielsen's own popular tunes like 'The Stone-breaker' and 'Thou Danish Man'.

After the 'Sinfonia espansiva' followed three more symphonies. In them the radicalization of the musical language is carried on, and they may also be said to evince a continued growth of imagination and a wider spiritual outlook—at least as far as No. 4 and No. 5 are concerned. But the 'Espansiva' has, even apart from the first movement, which is perhaps the most succesful in all Nielsen's symphonies, altogether a quite peculiar charm, mainly due to the healthy optimism and strong vitality that is expressed in this work; and it seems to be the most popular of all Nielsen's symphonies, the one that speaks most strongly and immediately even to the lay listener.

While each of the first three symphonies had been written after a pause of about ten years, it was only three years after the completion of 'Sinfonia espansiva' in 1914, that Nielsen felt inspiration and strength to start work on his next symphony, 'The Inextinguishable'. Apart from the violin concerto there is only one single major work from the period between these two monumental works, the *Sonata No. 2 for Violin and Piano,* op. 35, composed in 1912. Being a true link between the two symphonies, the work has features that point backwards as well as forwards. Traditional as to formal outlines, with three movements in the order: *Allegro—Adagio—Allegro,* the sonata at the same time marks a long step in the direction of a more progressive style, noticeable in the musical language, and especially in its relation to tonality. It was originally stated that the work was in G minor, but G minor is just about the only key that is not used in it—the first movement, for instance, ends in the key of E flat major, and the finale begins in B flat major and ends in C major. Even harmony is treated more daringly than before, especially the contrapuntal pattern causes a considerable increase in the number of polytonal passages.

The tonal freedom comes out clearly in the two opening bars of the first subject in the *first movement*—while the violin soars quickly from G minor to

A flat minor, the piano emphasizes the A flat tonality right from the beginning, which makes the D of the violin sound together with the D flat of the bass:

Ex. 24

Nielsen's ability to "let one thing grow out of another" is not absent from this work, either. For instance, in the continuation of the material from the first subject the following *cantabile* passage appears:

Ex. 25

out of which grows the lyrical second subject:

Ex. 26

Apart from this, sharp conflicts find expression in the development of the movement, where delicate lyrical passages alternate with others of a violently agitated character, leading in the end to a mood of serenity.

After the beautiful and solemn, extremely expressive *second movement, Molto adagio*, a certain relaxation is introduced in the *finale, Allegro piacevole*, written in free rondo-form, with the slightly waltz-like first subject:

Ex. 27

It returns in varying keys, separated by episodes in which the first movement is effectively reviewed by quotations from its thematic material.

Symphony No. 4, which—as mentioned above—was begun in 1914, was finished soon after New Year 1916. Like No. 2 and No. 3—'The Four Temperaments' and 'Sinfonia espansiva'—No. 4 has a title, namely 'The Inextinguishable'. By way of explanation Nielsen has written the following words in the score: "By using the title 'The Intextinguishable' the composer has tried to suggest by a single word what music alone has the power fully to express: the basic will to life. Music *is* life, and, like life, inextinguishable; so the title which the composer has given to his work may seem superfluous. He has employed it, however, in order to underline the strictly musical nature of his task. Not a 'programme' but a 'finger-post' pointing into the field of music itself."

In another connection Nielsen has singled out *movement* and *sound* as the fundamental manifestations of life and drawn the conclusion that music alone is able to reflect life directly, without paraphrasing it into abstract ideas. It is quite possible to accept this view, but on the other hand it appears that Nielsen himself must have doubted the necessity of the title chosen, for if there is no 'programme', why then have a 'finger-post'? And if music is life in the sense that Nielsen adopts here, then any work of music might, indeed, with the same right be called 'The Inextinguishable'. The fact that the idea which the work originates in, seems somewhat hazily formulated, has not, however, in any way marred its musical qualities. Already when it made its first appearance it was hailed by the critic Charles Kjerulf as "a masterpiece towering right into the skies", and it has kept this position to the present day.

Like the three preceding symphonies No. 4 consists of four movements, in this case in the following order: *Allegro—Poco allegretto—Poco adagio quasi andante—Allegro*. But while each single movement in the earlier symphonies had formed a separate whole in the classical manner, they are now linked together by connective passages, a technique that is known from several romantic symphonies, for instance Mendelssohn's 'Scotch'. The fact that the work contains a musical idea, the second subject in the first movement, which becomes the mainstay of the whole symphony, is, however, of greater consequence for the general effect, since this theme, having been left out in the recapitulation, breaks in once more in the finale and then provides the ultimate climax of the whole work; at the same time it yields thematic material in various ways for the two intermediary movements. As mentioned above the principle of a thematic breaking through had been anticipated in a remarkable way by Nielsen himself in his suite for strings in A minor, op. 1. What was portended by this early work has thus been brought to full artistic development in 'The Inextinguishable'.

In its idea, then, as well as in its form, the symphony has noticeable affinities with late romantic music, not least in the climaxes followed by a slackening, or sometimes an almost total dying away, which characterize most of the thematic groups in a way reminiscent of Bruckner. Altogether the mixture of strongly progressive and no less regressive features is more predominant than in any of the previous symphonies; indeed, it seems to be insisted on with almost demonstrative emphasis. After all, Carl Nielsen was born in the 60's and thus of the same age as composers like Sibelius, Mahler, Richard Strauss and Hugo Wolf. Taking into consideration, furthermore, that concurrently with his work as a composer he was a conductor at the Royal Theatre from 1908—14 and in the Musical Society from 1915—tasks bringing him into continual close contact with a great classical and romantic repertoire—it would have been something of a miracle if he had been able completely to avoid being influenced by this—in spite of all his creative originality. That 'The Inextinguishable' has been called Nielsen's stylistically least homogeneous work is not, I think, quite unjust. Passages of an extremely linear, occasionally almost atonal character are combined with purely homophonic stretches based on traditional major-minor tonality. The symphony cannot, however, be called eclectic in the proper sense of the word. No matter

38

where Nielsen has borrowed the material, consciously or subconsciously, it bears his own mark from beginning to end, appearing with an unmistakable, personal stamp even in the smallest details.

The *first movement* is characterized structurally by the tension between the aggressive first subject, gradually developed with unrestrained fierceness (ex. 28), and the naïve, pastoral second subject (ex. 29).

Ex. 28

Ex. 29

In the development, the most daring and at the same time the most imaginative Nielsen had written so far, this conflict is intensified to a dramatic struggle, in the last phase of which the second subject seems about to carry the day. The first subject, however, breaks in with full strength in the highly condensed recapitulation while the second subject tries in vain to find its form.

Between the first movement and the *adagio*, which is also full of tension, comes the idyllic *second movement*. The almost persistent writing in terms of chamber music makes this movement, dominated by the woodwind, seem perhaps a little out of place in a great symphonic work, but it is written in a charming manner with a fine and fastidious instrumentation. The first subject with the dropping thirds is evidently derived from the second subject of the first movement (ex. 29) —the basic idea of the symphony:

Ex. 30

The *third movement* may without hesitation be called the grandest slow movement Nielsen had written so far, afterwards surpassed as to intensity of expression only by the adagio in the first part of the fifth symphony. The movement, which puts an end to the preceding idyll with an abrupt gesture, is introduced by the highpitched violins in unison, playing an expansive melody accompanied only by heavy pizzicati in the deep strings supported by the kettledrum:

Ex. 31

After 16 bars the melody is taken up by the violas and cellos in an imitative reply, and this whole passage of 40 bars is now developed in a harmonically free and daring two-part counterpoint, unique in its kind within all symphonic composition till then, being, in fact, most closely related to old Netherlands polyphony. The tragic grandeur expressed in this magnificent subject—Nielsen himself compares it graphically with "an eagle riding on the wind"—gives way to the contemplative peace of the cantabile second subject:

Ex. 32

This leads, with increasing intensity of expression, into a sort of development, which by a contrapuntal use of motives from both subjects is gradually worked up to an almost stifling state of high tension, which is not released until the climax of the movement when the bright key of E major breaks in triumphantly. No proper recapitulation follows, only brief, fragmentary outbursts of the initial motive of the first subject, after which a sweeping string episode leads directly to the *finale*.

The beautifully modelled first subject, which, after a pointedly rhythmic introduction of seven bars, sets in, in the key of A major with a tinge of the Mixolydian mode, belongs to Nielsen's happiest musical ideas:

Ex. 33

It is carried on by the elastic triple time so characteristic of Nielsen, vigorously and as if breathing freely, but before long the primitive chaotic forces which had dominated the first movement break in again, by and by assuming the character of an impending natural catastrophe. This impression is heightened by the use of two pairs of *timpani*, producing a veritable thunderstorm, an element-ary rhythmic effect that astonished and started a discussion at the first perform-ance of the symphony. A slackening sets in; an impressive canon based on the first subject is spun out by muted strings, and suddenly, as if by magic, but perfectly organically worked into the context, the motive of thirds from the second subject of the first movement appears in the woodwind. The storm is brewing anew, again brought out by the infernal din of the kettledrums; but once revived the motive of thirds will not be ousted, and at last the whole subject comes together in an overwhelming E major *tutti* bringing the symphony to a triumph-ant close.

In 1918 Nielsen finishes the little work *Pan og Syrinx* "A Nature Scene for Orchestra", the inspiration for which came from the myth of Syrinx, who, flying from Pan, is eventually changed into a reed. This lyrical situation is rendered with a fine sense of atmosphere, including a tendency to pay more attention to timbre, a tendency that is borne out in the instrumentation, by the omission of the trombones and the additions to the percussion section (side drum, xylophone, glockenspiel, triangle, and tambourine). In this Nielsen evinces fairly close affinities with French impressionism, but at the same time he remains true to his nature, evidenced most clearly in his outstanding qualities as a melodist. This is a sidetrack, which he is to leave soon after. And yet, besides the steady development of the rhythmical and linear-contrapuntal aspects, there are signs of a growing sense of the purely sonorous qualities in his music of the following period. The possibilities of the individual instruments, particularly the wind, with regard to timbre and expression was a question to which he now paid much more attention than before.

In 1920 Carl Nielsen began working on the *Fifth Symphony,* which was finished just after New Year 1922. In this work he has almost completely broken away from the principles of form inherited from the classical composers, and has thus taken the decisive step towards a completely independent and personal treatment of form. Like all true innovators Nielsen realized that 'form' is not a fixed framework which may be filled with any 'content', but that form, on the contrary, in any given case emerges as the product of the material, its nature and qualities. The further he moved away from the classical principles of tonality, at the same time laying an ever increasing stress on the rhythmic-linear element, the more tenuous were the threads bound to be which still kept him tied to the classical forms.

How far this process of disengagement had advanced in the fifth symphony is seen in the form of the work as a whole. The cycle of four movements has given way to a form of two movements, or rather to a division into two great *parts.* The first part in its turn is divided into two mutually contrasting sections: *Tempo giusto* in common time, and *Adagio non troppo* in three-four time. These two are organically connected, however, in that an essential part of the material from the first section is contrapuntally combined with the material of the second section. The second part of the symphony is divided into four main sections: *Allegro 3/4—Presto 3/4—Andante un poco tranquillo C—Allegro 3/4.* Each two of these are linked together by bridge passages, so that the whole part sounds like a sort of concentrated cycle. As, however, the last *Allegro* is a free recapitulation of the first, and the intermediary passages are based on transmuted material from the same source, there are traces of the sonata form as well as the variation form.

As for the idea behind this symphony, it seems closely related to the preceding, 'The Inextinguishable'. The basic impulses seem to stem from the same idea of the struggle for life, the eternal conflict between constructive and destructive forces. But while the fourth symphony was concerned with the fundamental will to life, there is in the fifth a noticeable shift of the perspective from the biological approach to the social, in the widest sense of the word—the conflict, the tension between barbarism and civilization, between chaos and order. If possible there is even less evidence, however, of any propensity in Nielsen to write programme

41

music than there was in 'The Inextinguishable'—the fifth symphony has neither a title nor an 'explanation'; the music speaks for itself, but it certainly speaks with such suggestive force that there is no need for a 'translation'.

While the ideas behind the work are based on the fourth symphony, the music of the first part shows clearly that also works like 'Pan og Syrinx' and 'Aladdin' had gone before, especially the use of a very comprehensive percussion section, in which the side drum with its inciting rhythmic ostinato plays a prominent part.

Part One. The manner in which the *Tempo giusto* section opens the work is in itself a new departure in Carl Nielsen's symponic writing. While the first four symphonies open with a *tutti* entry, either on a chord or in unison, No. 5 starts *piano* with a peculiar hovering tremolo of thirds in the violas, and it is not until the fifth bar that something begins to happen:

Ex. 34

This whole section seems like the fantastic improvisation of a rambling imagination, made up as it is from a great many different, partly contrapuntally juxtaposed motives—from quite elementary rhythmic or figurative ones to such as are unfolded in sweeping melodious curves. The following two motives are particularly significant for the further development of the symphony—the second of them dominated by the side drum—as they are both taken up as the 'disturbing' elements in the *Adagio*:

Ex. 35

Ex. 36

The whole of this section is built up during one long crescendo and decrescendo, the expansive climactic passage of which takes the form of a march that grows more and more wild, seconded by the diabolic rhythm of the side drum. There is great tonal and harmonic freedom, hardly any traces of traditional harmony remain, and yet there is no question of atonality. The deepest tonal foundations are first an F, then, rising by fifths, a C, and finally a G, in which initially unambiguous tonality the *Adagio* sets in.

While the *Tempo giusto* section is an unmistakable symbol of primitive, chaotic barbarism, the *Adagio* section marks an abrupt transition to an entirely different world, a world of clarity, harmony, order. Now follows, flowing from this beautiful, melodious, diatonic subject:

Ex. 37

an impressive, sonorous rising, founded on polyphony, which culminates in a stirring, glorious B major. After a slackening *diminuendo* the subject sets in again, but almost immediately a disturbing factor turns up in the woodwind, the motive Ex. 35 from the *Tempo giusto* section. It pushes forward with increasing urgency, trying doggedly—alternating between woodwind and strings—to quell the *Adagio* melody, which is fighting for its life in the brass section. The tension reaches its critical peak after the side drum has entered the stage once more, seconded rhythmically by the trumpets—the struggle between the two opposite tendencies, the destructive and the constructive, is fought out in broad daylight now. At length comes the release. The G major, which had been drowned in a polytonal confusion, is re-established, and the *Adagio* subject breaks in triumphantly. The music fades away in a *cadenza* for solo clarinet, accompanied by the side drum, which vanishes in the distance. And all is silence.

The complete mastery of the purely musical development is not the least admirable feature of this grandiose movement,—the way in which all this variegated, apparently disparate material has been joined together, so that it forms a completely organic, magnificent whole. It seems so finished, so self-contained that the continuation in the second part of the work might seem less requisite from an aesthetical point of view. The dying away of the first part has been characterized as a 'nirvana', a view that emphasizes the complete release of tension. But does there not after all, properly perceived, remain a slight tension? The rounding off on the fifth of the G major chord, introduced by a rising third, is definitely an interrogatory phrase that can be traced right back to the dramatic recitative of the baroque:

Ex. 38

A question demands an answer, and the answer is given in the *second part* of the symphony. It is, in Simpson's interpretation, "the regenerative energies of man" we are now faced with; and the *Allegro* subject takes us immediately right *in medias res* with a resounding *tutti*:

Ex. 39

This subject literally surges along over the *ostinato* fourth motive in the bass, in the elastic three-four time so characteristic of Nielsen. There is an immense impelling energy in this first section, which seems bent on clearing away all barriers. The ensuing scherzo-like *Presto* takes the form of a fugue that is gradually whipped up to a tumultuous uproar, the subject of which is felt to be related to the *ostinato* bass motive of the *Allegro* (cf. ex. 39):

Ex. 40

43

Ebbing away at last into a state of complete languor this passage leads directly into the *Andante*, which introduces another fugue developing a subject that is based on that of the *Allegro*, but with alterations in time and tempo:

Ex. 41

a process which changes what was originally indomitable fierceness into lofty contemplation. The subject is developed in a sonorous texture dominated by the strings—a piece of 'inspired polyphony' unequalled in all recent music. Towards the end, in a highly expressive string passage, are heard the outlines of a subject which had appeared as a sort of second subject in the *Allegro*:

Ex. 42

a theme which is a less tense and more harmonious offshoot of the initial subject. In the ensuing recapitulation of the *Allegro* section ex. 42 at length turns out the leading idea of the second part of the symphony—in this respect analogous with the second subject of the first movement of 'The Inextinguishable'. The primitive, destructive forces, which had apparently been quelled in the first part, but which had by no means refrained from stirring in the second part, stand unmasked as the 'disturbing' element in the *Adagio* of the first part, when the coda sets in—alternating in the same manner between woodwind and strings while the kettle-drum with the rhythmic, vigorously pounding pedal point has now taken over the part played by the side drum. All the while ex. 42 fights its way into the brass section, breaking through triumphantly at length and thus bringing the whole work to its glorious close. This makes the connection with the first part quite patent, and any doubt of the vital necessity of the second part from a psychological point of view is at the same time cleared away.

With the fifth symphony Nielsen reached the absolute summit of his creative power, not only in his symphonic, but in his instrumental music altogether. Nothing that was added afterwards equals it in greatness of mind, vision, and imagination. The question is then if the following decade, the last of his life, marks a decline in his creative power. Generally speaking this is no doubt putting it too strongly, even if it is difficult to ignore certain signs of weakening. Two things should be borne in mind in this connection. First his heart trouble, which from now on impaired his physical energy for long periods. Secondly, that the inclination to experiment, which had never been alien to his frame of mind, became more pronounced now and brought him into direct contact with the international modernism of the 20's, a trend that was not, after all, quite in keeping with his own nature. This influence is particularly noticeable in the sixth symphony, which was finished in 1925.

Between this last symphonic work from Nielsen's hand and the fifth symphony there is, however, a piece of chamber music of a special character, written in 1922, the *Quintet for Flute, Oboe, Clarinet, Horn, and Bassoon*, op. 43. This was not his first attempt at chamber music for wind instruments; it was preceded by the little, humorous *Serenata in vano* for clarinet, bassoon, horn, cello and double-bass (1914). Even the wind quintet—with the movements: *Allegro ben moderato, Menuet, Praeludium* and *Tema con variazioni*—is chiefly diverting, a charming piece of music, full of freshness and good humour, which only in the prelude to the variations gives way to demoniacal ravings which seem almost like a reflection of the immediately preceding fifth symphony. Nielsen's interest in the characteristics of the various instruments, which had apparently been roused in 'Pan og Syrinx', stands out clearly in the wind quintet, especially in the variations based on his own melody to the hymn "My Jesus, make my heart to love Thee", in which each of the five instruments is made to reveal its particular quality of timbre and expression, now playing together, now separately.

In the *Sixth Symphony*, written in 1924—25, Carl Nielsen resumes a form-at-large of four separate movements: I. *Tempo giusto,* C, II. *Humoresque (Allegretto),* 2/4, III. *Proposta seria (Adagio),* C, IV. *Tema con variazioni (Allegro),* 2/4; the first and last movements are expansive, whereas the two brief movements in between are a sort of intermezzi. Apart from the finale there is practically no trace of the classical formal patterns; the work is, indeed, in several respects marked by a stylistic reorientation. This is seen partly in a further radicalization in the treatment of tonality and harmony, partly—and not least—in his attitude to tone and sound. What Nielsen had already achieved in chamber music when he wrote the wind quintet—the unfolding of the peculiar character of each single instrument or group of instruments—he now attempts to carry out in an orchestral work. It is true that the orchestration as such is still 'great' and with an extended percussion section as in the fifth symphony, but the *tutti* is only employed sporadically in the first and last movements, and discarded entirely in the intermediary movements in chamber-music style. The whole work may thus, in fact, almost be classified as a chamber symphony.

Carl Nielsen himself named the work 'Sinfonia semplice', and at an early stage of the planning of this work he had cherished ideas about music of a simple, light, and idyllic nature. The symphony as a whole does not, however, give this impression. It is true that the diverting element is predominant in the *Humoresque* as well as in the variations of the finale, but this is counterbalanced by the high seriousness and emotionality that prevails in the other two movements, expecially in the intensely expressive *Adagio*. The *Humoresque* in particular was a hard nut to crack when the symphony made its first appearance, with its many strikingly grotesque ideas, such as a repeatedly occurring trombone *glissando*. Was this meant seriously, or was it irony—and if so, was it perhaps a parody of certain extremist tendencies in contemporary music?

Even to-day it is difficult to give a definite answer to this question, and altogether the sixth is generally considered the weakest of all Nielsen's symphonies. It is fruitless to wonder how a seventh symphony would have turned out if he had had time and strength for yet another symphonic work. In the very last year of his life Nielsen did, however, finish another indisputably great work—the organ work 'Commotio', which in many ways calls the earlier symphonies to mind, by its grandiose tone and its stamp of more immediate inspiration. Would it have remained an isolated phenomenon, or did it mean that Carl Nielsen had started on his way 'back home'? The answer to this question was buried with him.

(Translated by H. Nørgaard and
N. Bugge Hansen)

THE CONCERTOS

by

Herbert Rosenberg

Nielsen wrote three concertos in all: a Violin Concerto (1911), a Flute Concerto (1926) and a Clarinet Concerto (1928). The first of these is quite easily understood, while the two late compositions are rather difficult. Like all other works dating from Nielsen's maturity the Violin Concerto takes its place within a common European classicistic tradition without renouncing a distinct individuality. Cognate individual traits also appear in the two late concertos, but the classicistic affinities are now pushed into the background by the influence of the 'modernisms' of the twenties. What makes the two concertos more difficult to grasp is, however, not so much this stylistic reorientation—manifesting itself e.g. in an unmistakable disintegration of tonality—as the fact that they are definitely works of the composer's old age, that is to say, they are written by an extremely experienced composer who knows how to avoid inessentials. That is why they open up only to those who have mastered them in detail.

The *Violin Concerto*, op. 33, a genial work written with great gusto, consists of two movements:

1. Præludium (*Largo*). *Allegro cavalleresco.*
2. *Poco adagio.* Rondo (*Allegretto scherzando*).

Although the work has only two movements, its construction is traditional in so far as two quick movements encompass a slow middle section—the latter not an independent movement, however, but only an intermezzo. But it is contrary to normal practice—though not to that of Nielsen—that the first and last movements are not in the same key (G major—D major). Both movements comply with normal ideas of form, the first taking that of a sonata, the second that of a rondo. In both cases the course of the music is highly stringent; but that Nielsen had the ability to compose cogently without the aid of stereotyped form schemes is evident from the slow intermezzo of the concerto and still more from its *Præludium.*

The latter begins exlposively and passionately making intensive preparations for a lovely theme (ex. 1), the meditative nature of which endows the music with a hopeful character, till a surprising turn of the remote key of C sharp major (bar 24) prepares the way for a tightening filled with expectation—e.g. by means of a dialogue between the solo violin and the orchestra—ending in an abbreviated

Ex. 1

and modified recapitulation of the theme Ex. 1 (bar 37). This is no soothing conclusion, however; on the contrary, it is a last preparation for the *allegro,* as the drum roll in the two last bars of the *Præludium* makes abundantly clear.

As a striking contrast the 'chivalresque' main theme of the *Allegro*

Ex. 2

enters immediately, introducing a movement that follows the classic sonata form so closely and clearly that we may save ourselves the trouble of a detailed analysis. Suffice it to say that the subsidiary theme of the movement (bars 53—72, resp. 225—244)

Ex. 3

reappears in a modified version as the epilogue of the exposition (bars 85—112), resp. the recapitulation (bars 253—267), and that the development section, culminating in the soloist's *cadenza,* is made up exclusively from the second subject and the 'cackling' motif

Ex. 4

so characteristic of Nielsen, which appears for the first time in the exposition when in bar 73, following the second subject, a fresh impetus is needed.

The Intermezzo begins gropingly and dreamily in a kind of D minor:

Ex. 5

The hesitant and tonally fluctuating interplay between the solo violin and the orchestra (here treated as a chamber orchestra) is terminated gently but un-

48

equivocally in A major by a new theme-like idea. Finally, the coda (bars 56—73) makes use of the material of Ex. 5 in preparing the ground for the finale. The very simple course of the latter may be concentrated into the following table:

Bars	1–31	32–43	44–83	84–91	92–109	110–149	150–157
	A	a	B	a	A	C	a
	D major		G minor		D major	B flat major	

158–304	305		306–321	322–329	330–345	346–371
A (Development)	solo cadenza		A	a	B	x
A major			D major		G minor	

372–410
Coda
D major

The rondo theme, A

Ex. 6

is highly characteristic of Nielsen, especially the third bar. It is presented twice by the solo violin, the two statements being separated by a middle section deriving from the third bar of the rondo theme. The same derivative is found as accompaniment to a canonically introduced motive of a connective nature,

Ex. 7

utilized for the bridge passages marked *a* in the table. B and C are the easily recognizable episodes of the finale. After the second episode *a* leads very quickly to a recapitulation of the rondo theme in A major, thus introducing a development section. In bar 174 the third bar of the rondo theme is changed into:

Ex. 8

and developed almost like a third episode. Then the main theme turns up again, beginning a passage of increased tension that is checked by the lurking theme:

Ex. 9

49

which is also treated like an episode (bar 232). Note the fragments of the main theme appearing in the accompaniment of Ex. 9. They soon come to the front, and from now on the dynamic development is given free scope, culminating in the solo *cadenza* of the movement.

The remainder of the finale speaks for itself. It is worth notice, however, that the bridge passage between the restatement of episode B and the coda, marked *x* in the table, is based on the motive derived from the main theme, Ex. 8. Furthermore, it must be pointed out that the coda begins as a last restatement of the rondo theme.

In contradistinction to the large orchestra of the Violin Concerto the *Flute Concerto* (no opus number) demands only a chamber orchestra where the string quintet has been supplemented with 2 oboes, 2 clarinets, 2 bassoons, 2 horns, 1 bass trombone, and kettledrums. The work has two movements:

1. *Allegro moderato.*
2. *Allegretto. Adagio ma non troppo. Allegretto. Poco adagio. Tempo di marcia.*

The first movement begins in D minor with an introduction that soon becomes tonally fluctuating; in bar 12 it is succeeded abruptly by the main theme in E flat minor:

Ex. 10

The two initial bars of the theme are repeated five times in all in more or less modified and expanded form and in varying keys, and after the first repetition an interpolated passage heightens the tension. With its major third the last repetition but one (strings in unison) serves as an announcement of the termination of the theme group while the last recurrence (on the flute) is transformed into a bridge passage leading to the subsidiary theme:

Ex. 11

After a *tutti* in F major this is followed (bar 37) by a concertino-like repetition for flute, clarinet and bassoon. Then a fresh tutti, dominated by the flute, begins to blur the outlines of the theme. From bar 52 onwards the turn-like conclusion of the subsidiary theme (the last six notes of Ex. 11) is used as the motive of the epilogue, only reduced to semi-quavers, and then follows the first solo-*cadenza* of the movement (bars 59—69) for a concertino-group consisting of flute and clarinet, with interposed remarks by the first violins.

The development begins in bar 70 in C major. In the course of a few bars the *stretto* of the second subject succeeds in building up a considerable tension,

50

culminating in a thematically independent, sharply contrasting section in D-Dorian for a solo group consisting of flute, trombone and kettledrum, the last mentioned instrument competing with the strings. The next section of the development begins in bar 97, tonally fluctuatingly, with the main theme. Fugally developed it reaches a climax in bar 101 and is succeeded by a slowly ebbing passage in E major, accompanied by the wind in unison. In bar 110 the soothing *cantabile* motive of the wind instruments is taken over by the solo flute:

Ex. 12

which in bar 122 takes up an expectant variation of the main theme, whereupon a solo *cadenza* (bar 133) for flute, ending in E major, leads on to the restatement. This is treated very freely. The first subject is recapitulated with entries in F minor by the lower strings followed by the upper strings, and after 12 bars comes a solo *cadenza*, the first half of which rests on a pianissimo drum roll in B flat. The second half is accompanied by the clarinet, ultimately reinforced by the bassoons; it serves to introduce the restatement of the second subject (bar 157) in G flat major, in which key the movement remains. Only six bars later the second subject is succeeded by the epilogue, derived from the soothing motive Ex. 12, the minor third of which, however, has been replaced by a major third in accordance with its concluding function. After a few ingeniously inventive bars the coda sets in (bar 179), based on a version of the second subject.

Although the final G flat major is the relative key of the initial one of E flat minor, it does not have a very calming effect, probably because D minor and F major have been so much in evidence. Consequently, a second movement is needed. The structure of this is outlined in the following table:

Bars	2/4 *Allegretto*			3/4 *Adagio*	2/4 *Allegretto*			3/4 *Adagio*
	1–11	12–28	29–61	62–92	93–114	115–129	130–137	138–144
	X	A	Y	B	A	Y	X	B

6/8 *Tempo di marcia*						
145–160	161–174	175–179	180–194	195–199	200–230	231–237
A′	Z	A″	C	A′	C′	A‴

X denotes an introduction, the keen B flat minor of which is softened by the G major of the idyllic rondo theme, A:

Ex. 13

Y is a connecting passage that becomes more sharply outlined in bar 39:

Ex. 14

In bar 62 it is replaced by the vividly contrasting episode, B, a tonally fluctuating passage with a melodious theme:

Ex. 15

presented in turn by the flute, the lower strings, and—in an abbreviated form—by a bassoon. After that a terse but very intensive *stretto* presentation of its first motive rounds off this section. Next, a recapitulation of the rondo theme is followed by the bridge passage Y in a modified version, succeeded by a varied, contrapuntally enriched repetition of the introduction X, serving to increase the tension. Now a retarding passage is interposed in the shape of a summary re-statement of the episode B, and after that the E major 'finale' of the movement begins: a pleasant and cheerful version of the rondo theme in 6/8 time, turning into the free continuation Z. A'' is a grotesque variation of A', while the *cantabile* section C, formed like a period, is in the nature of a fresh episode, after which comes a brief recapitulation of A' by the trombone. The coda of the finale begins with section C', the calming effect of which is heightened by the coda theme of the first movement, re-introduced by the trombone and brought to a conclusion by a burlesque *glissando*, the first of a whole series of *glissandi* on the trombone ultimately putting a final stop to the break-up dance of the coda, A'''.

The *Clarinet Concerto*, op. 57 was Carl Nielsen's last great orchestral work. With a little ingenuity it may be regarded as consisting of four movements, played *attacca*:

1. *Allegretto un poco. Allegro non troppo. Più allegro. Tempo I.*
2. *Poco adagio.*
3. *Allegro non troppo. Poco più mosso. Adagio.*
4. *Allegro vivace. Poco adagio. Allegro.*

The string quintet of the small orchestra is supplemented only with 2 bassoons, 2 horns, and a side-drum that plays a very important part in almost the whole concerto.

The first movement begins fugally with a jovial theme on cellos and basses:

Ex. 16

imitated by violas and bassoons and subsequently by the clarinet, that speedily leads into a free continuation (bar 22), ending in bar 33 where the strings begin an energetically pushing connecting passage, also developed as a *fugato*. Thus a growth in tension is initiated, culminating in bar 62 with the entry of the side-drum. The music now becomes filled with a sense of suspense, relieved in bar 79 by the clarinet that introduces the second subject:

Ex. 17

which dominates the scene till bar 96. Here begins another bridge passage, from bar 102 employing a theme of its own, accompanied by a busily pottering *pizzicato* on the strings in unison. With a steady increase in tension this connecting passage leads to the big solo *cadenza*, bar 133, mainly based on the first bar of the first subject (cf. Ex. 16) and the above connective theme. The *cadenza* ends in a free, shortened recapitulation, which after a gradual quickening of tempo (beginning in bar 163) turns into a bridge passage. A brief solo *cadenza*, accompanied by the side-drum, and an increasingly hesitant treatment of the initial motive of the main theme lead to the next movement.

The main theme of the second movement is heard on horns and bassoons and repeated a major sixth higher by the clarinet and the strings:

Ex. 18

From bar 236 onwards the dropping fourth followed by repeated notes (last bar of Ex. 18) acquires a constructive importance for the conclusion of the theme group. In bar 245 begins a lengthy display of dotted rhythms on the first violins, polyrhythmically accompanied by the second violins and the violas, and controlled by the heavily scored two-bar groups of the bass. Over the hurrying figures the clarinet sings an ecstatic tune, now and again suggestive of the initial motive of the concerto. When this remarkable section has drawn to its close, a fragmentary restatement (bar 283) of the *adagio* theme begins the transition to the third movement.

This movement, the longest of the concerto, serves the function of a scherzo. It is put in motion by a quiet melodic curve on the horns over an accompaniment of syncopated quavers. The main theme begins in bar 319:

Ex. 19

The third time this motive appears—now turned to the major—it is changed into a bridge passage, and brief, urgent figures gradually lead to a vigorously advancing section (bar 353), based on material drawn from the same theme. In bar 377 this passage gives place to the subsidiary theme of the scherzo:

Ex. 20

With its slower tempo this motive is epilogue-like as well as delaying; it is thus extremely usable, and it is, indeed, turned to the best account. First it is repeated by the clarinet (bar 385), but after a few bars the latter loses itself in soloistic flourishes that develop into a short dialogue with the orchestra. After that it is found in the lower strings (bar 397), occasioning another dialogue between the clarinet and the orchestra, only less acute. From bar 409 onwards reminiscences of it emerge in the strings, accompanying the clarinet that commences a quieting passage, and once more it is heard on the violins from bar 417, this time introducing the lyrically lingering entry of the clarinet at bar 425. In bar 433 the character of the music is altered: the interplay between the orchestra, still relying on remnants of the effective theme, and the fluttering figures of the clarinet becomes strenuously preparatory (note the aggressive manner of the side-drum). The goal is the section in 2/8 time (*Poco più mosso*) reached in bar 457 with a *pizzicato* presentation by the strings of still another variation of the same theme. This is followed (bar 463) by a diffusely spun out melody on the bassoon repeated by the clarinet (bar 485), and eventually transformed by the latter into a freely formed festoon of notes, culminating in the solo *cadenza,* bar 519. Now begins the transition to the finale with a number of hesitant recapitulations of the above-mentioned epilogue-idea of the *adagio*.

After two bars where the side-drum sets the pace, the finale is opened by the clarinet with the main theme:

Ex. 21

which is taken over by the basses and finally by the violins. Then the clarinet introduces the loosely built second subject (bar 558). At bar 592 there is a checking recurrence of the second subject of the scherzo, now turned into expectant triplets. Reaching the climax of the passage the clarinet delivers another deferring version of the same theme. Still more lingeringly the clarinet repeats this version as accompaniment to the main theme of the finale, that has turned up again on the upper strings. The main theme recurs in the minor, presented by an extremely brutal *fortissimo* on the violins, and once more the second subject of the scherzo appears at the highest pitch of the clarinet (bar 645). Then the movement loses itself in an expectant *pianissimo*.

In bar 665 the clarinet begins preparations for the conclusion of the finale by quoting the above epilogue theme of the *adagio*, followed by a quite enchanting variation of the main theme of the finale on the strings:

Ex. 22

Now the time has come to tackle the coda, principally based on the first subject of the finale. Gradually the sound fades away and the flow of the music becomes more quiet, till at last a few tender flageolet chords put a final stop to the work.

(Translated by Holger Nørgaard)

THE PIANO WORKS

by

ARNE SKJOLD-RASMUSSEN

Carl Nielsen's attitude to the piano never became pianistic seen in relation to the great romantic piano literature. Some features in Nielsen carry the stamp of the piano style of Brahms but by and large we must acknowledge that in the "Chaconne" and "Theme with Variations" Nielsen has created a Danish style of piano music which is unlike anything else.

Nielsen spent much time at the piano. When very young he studied Bach's "Wohltemperiertes Klavier" on his own. In the course of his studies at the Academy of Music he obtained such skill that later he composed almost everything at the piano. As the fruits of his relation to the instrument he has given us five great works and several smaller compositions for the piano.

A span of almost forty years intervenes between the composition which was published first and that which came last. At long intervals he turned directly to our instrument, creating works which often shocked his contemporaries. To-day these works appear as fully clarified; they can be analyzed throughout, but they have lost none of their freshness in the course of time, rather the opposite. Tenaciously and slowly they have won for themselves a position in the repertoires of Danish pianists, several of whom have had a hand in breaking down the opposition which Nielsen's compositions sometimes met with abroad because of their special style and tone. Just let the process be slow and practically left to itself—their position will be secured.

To-day when Schönberg and Webern, or their principles, are often placed in the seat of honour it is interesting to notice that these gentlemen were not strangers to Nielsen; he reached out a hand to them in his last compositions for the piano, he marked their technique, digested it without giving up one bit of his own personality, and gave us his three last piano pieces, op. 59, which were also sprinkled with a little impressionism. They appear as Nielsen's most advanced work for the piano and can be difficult to interpret at first glance, but time and effort will bring them out as a work of art characterized by imagination and integrity.

As a teacher at the Royal Academy of Music I have for many years listened to the students'—my own and other teachers'—presentation of Carl Nielsen's piano compositions. With a teacher's desire for perfectionism in his students I have not always been persuaded that they have fully grasped the idea and the thread of his compositions (which are difficult for those who tackle them for the first time), but I have always been happy at the enthusiasm which they have expressed for the work. They have had a powerful artistic experience to which they will return and which they will go deeper into soon again.

Because Nielsen meant for me at the age of 17 the first experience of modern music under my own hands, it has been a constant thrill to watch the reactions of the students when they have rehearsed a couple of pages on their own. It sometimes happens that they are hesitant and at a loss as to the essentials of it; their faces are not lit spontaneously with enthusiasm. That is what happened to me.

I had just been to a final rehearsal of "Sacre" and had also heard "Mathis der Maler"; that was possibly why I thought that this Nielsen stuff was something half-modern. But when I discovered what a powder barrel I was handling I made it explode, and the piano went out of tune before its time, according to the Academy's budget. The fuse had been ignited and the dramatic elements in Carl Nielsen's music made the young blood forget the art of self-control.

Luckily something like this can also happen to the students of to-day, but it is often necessary to guide their steps away from their own time towards a spontaneous curiosity for sounds in nature and orchestra, and to a recognition of the fact that the drama in Carl Nielsen's music often is more original and direct than that in many other great composers (without disparagement!). This drama may literally stem from incidents which we do not think of as directly connected with music—the twig that breaks behind us in the dark forest and then the terror, the struggle between the tree and the wind, the conflict between the dog and his aggressive flea.

My teacher, Christian Christiansen, told me how he had asked Carl Nielsen to give him an idea of the degree of "molto patetico quasi parodico" on the last page of "Impromptu", op. 59. "That's quite simple," answered Nielsen, "think of a tipsy fellow trying to keep his dignity and upright position by holding on to a lamp-post!" That makes it clear to us how this passage should be played.

Carl Nielsen's point of departure in the piano compositions which were published first, op. 3, must have been the popular short romantic piano compositions of the time, such as the relatively easy songs without words by Mendelssohn and Schumann; with a Nordic tone: Hartmann, Gade and Grieg. Nielsen's op. 3 contains these ingredients, but they have a face of their own; in particular the "Arabesque" shows a new line. Here we find figures and ideas which were to be the basic principles of Nielsen's later piano style, the quickly torn-off demise-miquavers, the stubborn repetition of them, the abrupt accents, the hysterical, clarinettish melisma in bar 13, whose fingering hints that Carl Nielsen later on frequently would work at the piano in groups of notes which could be kept within the capacity of five fingers without having resort to passing fingering. In the same composition we learn about the melodic independence of the bass; it does not remain just an accompaniment and indication of harmony. Together with the figurations of the right hand it creates that kind of polyphony which in conjunction with the short note groups are decisive components of Nielsen's later piano music.

The first magnum opus for the piano is the "Symphonic Suite", op. 8, whose piano style has many points of resemblance to that of the young Brahms. In contrast to all of Nielsen's later piano compositions, which begin quietly with a gentle break of the silence, this work opens with a crash that lasts through the whole movement, aggressive to the ear-drums, but wonderful to take part in, sound and fury all the way, like a bath in the mountains of Norway.

When Busoni had expounded and played this suite to his students, Nielsen asked him whether any of them were now going to rehearse it and include it in their repertoire. "That can't be done," Busoni answered, "it is not orchestrated for the piano". And it is heavy work, even today when we pianists have taken upon us the presentation of many strange and often unpianistic recent and less recent works for the piano with our hands which still have got ten fingers only. As in the case of long episodes of the F minor sonata for piano by Brahms, Nielsen's suite is orchestral music, which has been adapted for the piano. This makes it difficult in places to bring it to euphonious life on the instrument.

The passages where we fall short are such ones as the long episodes of forte. What is described as a stable volume of sound in "Intonation" can be made lighter and more inviting by accentuating the highest note in the right hand chords and shading the quality of the bass accordingly. This reduces the entire level to the advantage of the melody; the movement becomes more euphonious without losing any of its enormous intensity.

Ex. 1

It is a good exercise to play the violin sonata in A major, op. 9. Here we are bound by the violin's capacity of tone. If we go beyond this on the piano it does not make good chamber music. We have a wealth of notes in the piano part, many of them forte and fortissimo; temptation may become too strong: the hundred and twenty horse-power of the concert grand as opposed to the fifteen of the violin leaves us no other possibility than to make the sound supple and differentiate the parts.

Ex. 2

The following passages are impossible to manage because the bass notes cannot be held at full length by the pedal without obscuring the texture too much:

Ex. 3 and 4

Op. 8, 3rd movement

Op. 9, 2nd movement

Concerning the example from the A major sonata (including the three following bars and corresponding passages of the finale) I have made an experiment at a broadcasting presentation, trying to overcome the difficulties by making the person who turned over the leaves play the deep notes which cannot possibly be sustained by hand or pedal. I have not had the courage to try this in the concert hall, but it was exciting to hear these passages played exactly as prescribed by Nielsen.

On pages 11, 12, and 13 in the third part of "Symphonic Suite" are found enormous stretches of crescendo and forte, which can be tiring to both the performer and the listener if we do not give way and reduce the sound a little in order to bring it up to the full again at the peak rather than strain the instrument. From the top and right down to the bottom of page 12 a variation of tone can be obtained by continuously introducing light and shade into the counterpoint, while the theme can be more stable in tone. At the top of page 13 where all the music has turned into counterpoint the two hands should play differently as regards sound, that is to say subdued where the triplets begin.

Ex. 5 and 6

In the presentation of a work like the "Symphonic Suite" all our efforts towards making it as pianistic and euphonious as possible imply that it is the rich timbre and great legato of the orchestra we dream of when we let some parts recede in favour of others, or when we shade a chord by accentuating one or more of the notes.

60

Probably it is very much a matter of personality to what extent pianists, more or less consciously, colour their performance according to their musical imagination or according to the style and character of the compositions on the music-rest. As long as the movement is swift and translucent (e.g. a finale by Mozart) we are satisfied physiologically and musically; it is definitely piano music. Perhaps it is otherwise in the slow movement; we cannot make our material sufficiently expressive and beautiful in timbre because our notes fade away fairly soon after they have been struck. We are longing for an instrument which in this respect is more perfect, at any rate one which can sustain a note longer—and all other instruments, such as the flute or violin, are capable of this—and we adapt our shading of the melody and the other parts accordingly.

Owing to its many running semiquavers the last movement of the "Symphonic Suite" is the one most easily rendered on the piano; quite charming in its central idea, interrupted by the resumés, which probably should be played slightly faster than when they occur for the first time, so that the movement can keep its lovely flight.

The motto of the suite: "Ach, die zärtlichen Herzen! Ein Pfuscher vermag sie zu rühren," must be open to interpretation, but Nielsen must have been aware that with this piece of music he had settled with that side of the late-romantic music which he disliked.

The piano compositions, op. 11, show to what a high degree Nielsen now approaches the piano in his own manner; the above-mentioned 'handfuls' of notes without passing fingering come out more clearly here than in op. 3 and op. 8.

"The Top" circles on the spot within an ever-decreasing radius of the hand until the whip sets it moving again in somewhat wider circles. It keeps whirring, more furiously at each lash of the whip, until at last it tumbles over in a glissando. This character-piece must hold the record for avoidance of passing fingering. A few instances of this are indeed indicated, but some of them had better be left out. This composition is decidedly piano music and ought to be included in all piano schools for building up the egality of the five fingers.

"The Jumping Jack" (ex. 8) kicks so violently when the 'handfuls' occur that he is on the point of falling off the nail.

Ex. 7 and 8

Op. 11, No. 2   *Op. 11, No. 4*

The "Chaconne", op. 32, is a true renewal of Danish piano music. In this very strict form Nielsen has the instrument at such close quarters that he is forced to decide what really is feasible and to give up what is not, as e.g. the above-mentioned episodes of the violin sonata in A major and the "Symphonic Suite".

From slow note-values we glide into quicker ones, yet they offer no technical difficulties or peculiarities. On page 3 there are many episodes of scalic semiquavers—right up to 12 notes—where it is necessary to let the thumb pass under a finger two or three times, in accordance with the nature of the scale and not the beat of the music. On the same page we may see Nielsen's tendency to divide the materiel into groups, 'handfuls' (ex. 9).

Ex. 9 and 10

On the following pages this tendency gathers strength (ex. 10) but it is interrupted by similar figures, which require passing fingering, while the 'great' variations (pages 9—11) work quite peculiarly in a manner yet unheard-of on the piano. It was while Nielsen worked on these two variations that his wife, the sculptor, Anne Marie Carl Nielsen, left her studio in order to say to him, "This won't work, Carl, you must stop—you are overdoing it!" I understand her perfectly. When properly prepared through the preceding variations, this passage, the climax of the chaconne, makes so astounding an impact that it takes away one's breath by its dissonances and relentless rhythm. The material is felt to be of enormous coherence and length, but in technical detail it is unbelievably short, two strikings, one in either hand, constitute the technical group. Especially in its second phase this passage is difficult to play becuase of the often enormous distance between the demisemiquavers of the right hand and the melody far below.

Ex. 11

In the coda demisemiquavers form a counterpoint to the second theme of the chaconne. Quickly moving and strongly modulating they make up scales and patterns, not born in separate groups. Such groups turn up again on the last page in the shape of quintuplets.

We should be far from the assumption that this masterpiece owes its existence to the composer's imperfect mastery of the piano; in spite of Nielsen's inability to give his own composition an adequate presentation and in spite of his breaking new ground he has put his thoughts so effectively in the idiom of the piano

62

that such thoughts never cross our minds. Brahms's first piano concerto has often been abused on the grounds of being angular, because here Brahms has had to find yet unheard-of phrases and figures in order to cover the meaning of what he wanted to express and to make the piano a dynamic match for the orchestra. His concerto belongs to the world repertoire, and we play it with a joy as great—only different and of a more brow-wiping kind—as we do one of the piano concertos by Mozart. Our praise is due to any new figures that occur in a fine and beautiful context, if only by studying and absorbing them we can turn them into a familiar 'grip' on the instrument, then they have become accepted pianistically.

The often mentioned figure, generally of five notes, is a necessary means of expression for Nielsen, for it is to be found in great numbers in his work, even apart from his piano compositions, and it may have originated in any other place than the piano. Nielsen has often taken us by surprise with his curious and completely unconvential view of other instruments, for instance in the clarinet concerto and the wind quintet, eliciting from them some curious talk and a droll figure quite in harmony with the wood or metal which they are made of. Perhaps we can find points of likeness to sounds in nature; to a sudden ruffling of a calm surface; to the amusing and strange arabesques improvised by the wind-instruments of the orchestra before the concert; to the side drum being tested in half a roll to get the feel of the sticks in the hands. Had it been an artistic necessity to Carl Nielsen to employ seven or nine notes to obtain the intended effect, he would have done so.

"Theme with Variations", op. 40, is teeming with separate figurations, handfuls of notes; with few exceptions they completely fill this work, forming sentence after sentence.

Ex. 12 and 13

Variation 10.

Variation 6.

While the harmonies of the "Chaconne" emerge gradually as a result of the progression of the parts, in "Theme with Variations" they are established from the beginning, providing the foundation of the entire composition. Over the harmonies the variations are spun, mainly by means of arpeggios. Already in the second variation, the actual melody has disappeared; it does not reappear in its original shape until it forms the introduction of the second half of the work, and then there are changes, created from new harmonies. Nielsen's presentation of drama, lyricism and humour lies hidden in the theme: the bass comes after the treble and comments on the happenings up there, a play with possibilities has begun.

The bass must have a life of its own, the opposite of the treble, which is playing ; the left hand must sound and play 'in reverse': ⌐>⌐ . Variation 1 begins with a linking of the right and the left hand's idea from the theme; because of the left hand's original phrasing, there is good reason to let the high B be the most resounding note in the stanza. The two elements do the harmonic work beautifully between them. In the next variation, the relationship between them has become critical; there is a conflict, but they still recognize each other. But in Variation 4 they do not—the trumpets and the strings are fighting over the throne, and the first half of the work ends with Variation 6, where Nielsen lets the one element stubbornly stick to its centre of movement, which only changes location when the other element threatens to interfere. There is time for them to fight with the same weapons, and to exchange them, but by the time it becomes necessary for us to come to the rescue and separate them, they do not exist any more. Only a whiff of gunpowder in the nostrils indicates where it all took place. And the wait which follows until the work flows quietly on again is almost unparalleled in music.

Ex. 14

The variation is typical of the way of writing which consists of note-groups that can be 'held in the hand' (without passing fingering); the idea of the variation is repeated in an extreme form in Variation 13 which demonstrates such sadistic humour that it can be described by Schandorf's remark in the Carl Nielsen biography: "What a nerve!"

The work concludes with Variation 15, where the idea from Variation 6 and 13 is repeated, this time put to the piano with such violent dynamics that no one would be angry, if the piano failed to produce euphony; the struggle to stay within the bounds of the instrument's ability is difficult, the pressure from within is so great. Nielsen ends the movement with a diminuendo and a naturally growing rallentando which occurs in the note values; he writes quasi rall., in parantheses, similar to the ending of Brahms's Rhapsody in G minor. The choral is placed uppermost, the exhausted antagonist below; in the work so far the two elements have been equal in all attacks against each other, hereby keeping the excitement intact, but now we are really in some doubt. Compositionally speaking, they finish with the same weight as when they began in the theme, but I believe that the left ought to give way a little in tone to the right for the last 4 bars, so that light may prevail just a little.

In Carl Nielsen's Suite, op. 45, we meet his further developed piano style, plus certain traits of the impressionistic style. (A little pre-view is in Variation 12 of Theme with Variations). They are employed very gently, he sees possibilities in them, but doesn't linger, absorbs them and still writes à la Carl Nielsen. The polyphonic life, as we know it, especially from the two previous great works, is not influenced by these traits.

In the first movement, one hardly notices any new characteristics, but in the second, they are obvious, and contribute to a hovering, poetic atmosphere. Nielsen's music possesses an awareness of substance to a far greater extent than that of the impressionists, and this must manifest itself in the performance. In the case of Ravel, the figure furnishes a background colour (ex. 15), with Nielsen they are both ground colour and melodic core (ex. 16) in that the notes B flat and A are part of a long melody and as such must be in the execution; there is in the matter itself opposition to being weakened completely. At the top of page 10 (ex. 17) the semiquavers must of course yield to the two melodic elements, but they must not be indistinct in the striking, so that they only form one third, with vibrations; they constitute the rhythmic path, and each step must be a conscious one.

In the corresponding place in the finale (ex. 18) the same is true; albeit weak, the Gs must not lose their intensity, in the presence of too great a sonority from the left hand.

Ex. 15 and 16

Ex. 17 and 18

The tone-groups, the 'handfuls' of notes are still there; they are neutralized to an organic whole. Rich and varied piano-playing on an advanced level is necessary to meet the challenges of the suite. If we show up with Brahms's great piano compositions at our finger-tips, we are quite well-prepared for playing the Suite; we would be even better equipped if we could boast the "Chaconne" and "Theme with Variations" in our repertoire. With its added new ideas and free from a traditional strict form, we have here a fantastic piano work, perhaps Scandinavia's greatest, which ought to appear on musical programs just as often as op. 40 and op. 32. The thinking in terms of orchestration discussed earlier is, in my opinion, most essential, especially in the Suite's third piece.

Nielsen's last large work for the piano is op. 59, the Three Piano Pieces which, with their mixed styles, were complicated for their time. Many thought that Nielsen had betrayed something in himself, but the next generation say No. We have now seen these pieces in their proper perspective, worked with them, listened to them and finally acknowledged Nielsen's readiness to defer to the pulses of the times and work them into his own material. To-day, we marvel at

65

the process which produced a true Carl Nielsen work. The scope of his mind has again encapsulated a new element. He couldn't bear Schönberg's style, but nevertheless he composes many bars in this work which consciously contain all 12 tones. As in impressionism, he has seen possibilities for renewals in the language of music and has translated thought into action.

The whole-tone technique, which the impressionists often used for creating atmosphere in a quiet, sometimes dim way, is used in the last piano pieces as a source of energy; swinging from one whole-tone complex to the other, we are on hazardous ground compared with earlier music of Carl Nielsen, but what does that matter? There is a breathless, dramatic strain over the fugal episode, his creative power is as great as it ever has been; it is hard to be on such a stormy sea. Finally, he fixes the rudder, tonally speaking, and after the storm his harbour will be E flat major. Is the ship battered? Perhaps, but it is *sailing*.

The piano technique further develops the phenomena from the three previous works. Now that we have reached the coping-stone of Nielsen's work for the piano, it strikes us that we are left with a very economical piano style. Fast, technical passages and motives and melodies are formed by using small intervals, so that they can be played in groups 'under the hand'; the connection between these takes place more often by moving the hand than by using meticulous passing fingering. The close, packed chords on the piano are related to those of Brahms.

Piano Music for Small and Big, op. 53, was written after a discussion in the Music Teachers' Association, where there was a crying need for simple, modern compositions for teaching purposes. Nielsen went right to work on the project with great zeal, and composed 24 short five-finger pieces in all keys. Many of them are excellent for children, mostly those that are funny, comical or grotesque, not merely because they dispense with passing fingering; others are better for adults—the thoughtful, soulful, and strange pieces. Here we get a cross-section of Nielsen's production, a long series of small works of art, covering the whole of Nielsen's wealth of emotions.

In the printed material by which coming generations shall inherit and study Nielsen, there is not sufficient order. To correct this situation is more important than to place the blame for something which is shameful to us all.

There are many examples of how nations have let important anniversaries be the occasion on which to publish their great artists' works in flawless editions. The 100th anniversary of the birth of Carl Nielsen ought to be that occasion, used by artists, critics, scholars, responsible publishers and authorities for the publication of revised editions of his works within all genres. So much more could be done if it were done immediately, in view of the fact that in our very midst are musicians who were close to Carl Nielsen, and who could participate in such a project with their whole heart: Thorvald Nielsen, Gilbert Jespersen, not to mention Emil Telmányi, who often was able to observe Carl Nielsen's

66

creative process closely, and who, in an exemplary way, has corrected some of his works.

Most of the printer's errors in the piano works are by now well-known among pianists; although it was not such a long time ago that strange things were heard in the concert hall in the 3rd Piano Piece of op. 59 due to incorrect indication of the key.

The numerous records with Nielsen's music have enormous significance in its popularization, but for a musician, the most important thing is to feel his music with the hands. For this, the existing four-handed editions of a few orchestral works have been of inestimable value, but many more could be made accessible if experts were commissioned to produce such transcriptions. Just imagine having Carl Nielsen's symphonies in eight-handed piano arrangements available at all conservatories and schools of music!

(Translated by Karen Stetting)

THE ORGAN WORKS

by

Finn Viderø

Only in the very last years of his life did Carl Nielsen take an interest in the organ. It is strange, after all, that he did not feel prompted to write for this instrument at an earlier date as his music often tends towards the polyphonic texture so well suited to the organ. This lack of interest which, by the way, Nielsen shared with several contemporary composers is no doubt due to the very subordinate position the organ occupied in the musical life of his time.

In the 17th century the organ because of its distinctive tonal qualities was entitled "Queen of Instruments" and was a centre of rich musical activity. After the latter half of the following century, however, it gradually lost the genuine organ sonorities substituting for them a rather poor imitation of the contemporary orchestra. As a result during the last third of the 19th century the organ was generally disregarded and attempts at rescuing it from oblivion by a series of concerts with contemporary romantic music hardly aroused any interest in the instrument or in its repertoire. Only with the re-discovery and restoration of the old Schnitger organ in the St. Jacobi Church in Hamburg about the middle of the nineteen-twenties was there a change and organ building was again concerned with building instruments of a true organ type.

The first signs of this reform movement, which has been of such importance for modern organ construction, showed up in this country at the end of the twenties. Judged by a modern standard, however, it was nothing but the first frail shoots of what would later bloom. Yet it was decisive, not because it met with any response let alone enthusiasm from organists, but because it drew the attention of musically interested people to the instrument bringing about a situation in which composers were expected to take the initiative in writing for the organ thus continuing an old tradition in a modern idiom.

Carl Nielsen needed only a hint from those immediately concerned and before long he had written a series of little preludes for the organ, 29 in all, which were published in 1930 as his opus 51. Two additional preludes of the same sort not published until 1947 (without opus number) were probably composed immediately after the first group, perhaps as the beginning of another series. The model for these little preludes which at most comprise 30 bars, occasionally coming near to an extreme brevity and even to perfunctoriness, Nielsen found in the classic organ music of Bach, Scheidt, Frescobaldi, Pachelbel and others which he studied in order to find out how best to write for the organ. The style of these small pieces is, of course, very much his own but it is really amazing how varied they are as to texture, form, tonal progressions and expressivity.

A few of them are made up of chord progressions only:

Ex. 1, The beginning of prelude no. 3.

Others use figured chords which generally are repeated in sequences at other pitch levels and sometimes modulate into remote keys to end up in the original key thus rounding off the form by a more or less strict repeat of the initial theme. Still others start off as a fugue with a unison theme imitated by the following voices but frequently the imitation is not strict and only occasionally is the theme answered in the dominant or used for a stretto as in an ordinary fugue:

Ex. 2, The beginning of prelude no. 10.

In some of the preludes the principal feature consists in keeping going a uniform mechanical rhythmic pattern (ex. 3) and here and there we find the stock phrases of Nielsen's style: horn fifths and reiterated repeats of the half-tone step or the minor third.

Ex. 3, from prelude no. 11.

The musical character is now graceful or lyric, now capricious or dramatic and sometimes reflects gravity and solemnity. Certainly these preludes are not church music even if some of them have later found their way into the church as preludes or postludes nor are they really suitable for instruction. The composer has not given any hints as to registration or dynamic shades, his agogic indications are few and the tempi which are suggested by metronome marks above the single pieces are altogether a little on the slow side but according to the composer's note the tempo should always be determined by the instrument and the acoustics. One gets rather the impression that these pieces were written not for

70

us but were made for his own sake. They are studies in organ texture with the purpose of trying out the various possibilities of the instrument. As a matter of fact several of them look like drafts for the work Nielsen may already have had in mind at this time and which he soon worked out: the large-scale fantasia *Commotio* that was to become his swan song. With this piece he succeeded not only in making himself entirely familiar with a genuine organ style but also in transferring essential features of Baroque music into a modern idiom. *Commotio* means movement, and Nielsen in order to emphasize the impersonal nature of the piece chose this title which says something essential about the generating force behind all music. While in his fourth symphony the will to life makes itself heard here the immanent force of the music finds vent in a constant flow, now increasing, now decreasing. Accordingly the piece is written in an entirely free form closely modelled after the toccata of the Baroque and like it made up of varying episodes, a constant current now of impetuous passages and tremendous chords:

Ex. 4a, the first three bars of "Commotio".

Ex. 4b, bar 21 and 22.

now of canonic or fugal sections:

71

Ex. 5a, bar 78—85.

Ex. 5b, bar 113—121.

and again of gently sounding melodies of a pastoral character:

Ex. 6, bar 441—449.

The single sections are bound together as an entity by little melodic turns emerging occasionally as it were here and there, now suggesting something immediately ahead, now recalling to memory something previously heard, a technique often used in the organ toccata of the 17th century and more especially that of Buxtehude.

Commotio falls into two sections like the prelude and fugue of the Baroque. The first section is of a more free, improvisatory character while the fugal episodes play a greater part in the second section even employing thematic transformation in the manner of the classic variation ricercar:

Ex. 7, bar 319—20 and 366—67.

The complex texture which in places is extremely difficult to play and the large dimensions of the piece (*Commotio* comprises 512 bars and takes about 22 minutes to perform) and its character of a mosaic made up of dissimilar sections in varying time signatures and keys make heavy demands on the player at the same time preventing the listener from getting a clear idea of the general structure of the form. This is to some extent also made difficult by the many tonal liberties

72

which the work abounds in. But in reality its fundamental tonal structure is rather simple. The first part of the piece may largely be regarded as based on what in the beginning declares itself as G minor but which later turns to G major as the dominant of C major, the persistent principal key of the second section. It is easy enough to analyze the form but an analysis does not say anything essential because the effect of the piece upon the listener very much depends on the way the single sections are linked together and how they develop out of each other.

There are no indications as to registration but the composer has suggested the fundamental character of each section—and the change it undergoes—by dynamic marks. Several times in the course of the piece we meet with tremendous climaxes followed by relaxation of the tension, a diminuendo leading to piano or pianissimo. These dynamic fluctuations prove that *Commotio* however well it may be written for the instrument cannot lay claim to be in every single detail in accord with the true nature of the organ as we find it in the classic organ music. The character of the piece is symphonic. Therefore, it cannot be regarded as a tribute to the organ reform movement as is sometimes maintained nowadays. The new trend was alien to Carl Nielsen and he never came to making up his mind about the questions arising out of a performance of his piece on an organ of classic type where every dynamic change is at the same time a change of color. He assumed that *Commotio* would be played on organs of the modified modern type which have now almost disappeared and given way to instruments of classic disposition. As a classic instrument does not generally possess the many varieties of tone color in 8- and 4ft. pitch which *Commotio* requires the dynamic suggestions of the composer will have to be adapted when the piece is performed on such an organ. The lesser dynamic changes within the single sections should be left out of account and emphasis placed on the contrast between clearly defined dynamic levels the tone color of which may most profitably be arranged as gradations of a basic stop combination.

(Translated by Finn Viderø
and Stephen Kahn)

THE DRAMATIC MUSIC

by

Jürgen Balzer

Carl Nielsen cultivated all the musical *genres* which were current in his day, but they fall at irregular intervals in his work. It is not to be wondered at that his interest in the organ was awakened relatively late in his career: he had no 'professional' links with it. Less natural, however, is the absence of string quartets in his work after his 41st year. His loss of interest in this medium is puzzling, the more so because in his compositions he develops a polyphony with stronger and stronger emphasis on the independence of the individual parts. It can perhaps be more easily explained that he takes leave of the opera at the same time, in 1906, for in no other *genre* are there more obstacles between the idea of the composer and its realization. The clearer the composer's idea takes shape before his inner eye, and the more he comes to master his means of expression, the more will he tend towards trying to realize this idea within the *genres* which offer the best conditions. And there is no getting round the fact that the way between the finished manuscript and the presentation of the work is longer and more arduous for opera than for chamber music and symphonies. In any case, this is true north of the Alps and also, but to a lesser extent, perhaps, in Italy; compare the testimonials afforded by Verdi, her greatest musical genius. But Verdi was *forced* to fight his way through these difficulties, he had no choice, for he was a dramatist. We cannot say the same about Nielsen, to him the opera was a sideline, and in his maturity the very essence in his art points in the direction of the symphony, as with Beethoven, Bruckner, and Sibelius.

Nielsen's interest in opera probably has to do with his connection with the theatre. From the autumn of 1889 to the end of June 1905 he played second violin in 'Det kongelige Kapel' (the orchestra of the Royal Theatre in Copenhagen) and both his operas (with the exception of the third act of 'Maskarade') were composed during this period, from his 33rd to his 41st year. This would seem to indicate a certain connection between his work as a musician and his desire to deal with the problems involved in writing operas.

Here it is interesting to note that in 1890, when he goes abroad on an Ancker scholarship, the opera violinist goes straight to Dresden, where he steeps himself in Wagner. The effect of this is intoxicating. The diary of the twenty-five-year-old composer overflows with eulogy of Wagner: "The music is magnificent! The musician who does not think Wagner great must be very small-minded." The 'Rheingold' inspired these words. 'Siegfried' gives rise to the following entry: "The first act is the manliest and most energetic music ever written!". To a friend he writes: "This week I have heard the whole Niebelungen Ring by Wagner. What a man! Great God, what a giant in our time. That there are people who don't like Wagner's music, that is inconceivable. I was not over-enthusiastic about him when I came here, but that must be because I only knew Tannhäuser and Lohengrin and some fragments of his later operas; but now I am at a loss for words which are strong enough for his praise. He is a towering genius. Hats off!"[1] A few days later, however, the diary bears witness that Nielsen had not left his critical faculty behind when he left Denmark: "I admire Wagner and am of opinion that he is the greatest genius of our century. But I don't like the way he spoon-feeds his audience. Every time a name is mentioned—though its bearer may be dead and buried many years ago—we are given his 'leitmotif'. I find this very naïve and it has a somewhat comical effect on me."[2]

From Dresden he goes to Berlin, where he hears 'Die Meistersinger': "How fascinating this opera is! I wonder if it isn't Wagner's best work. Is it not more thoroughly healthy than the later operas? I think it will live longest, but I cannot explain why. It is just a feeling I have. If I were to express in one word what I feel when I think of this opera, I should say: *ruddy*."[3]

Those who are familiar with Nielsen's later writings will probably recognize the word 'healthy'. Already when he was twenty-five, then, Nielsen found music more or less 'healthy', and we know that he finished up reacting against certain tendencies in Wagner's music as 'unhealthy'.

In the main it was the 'method' Wagner used in his musical dramas he reacted against in his youth, and this reaction grew stronger as the years went by. In the autumn of 1894 he went abroad again on a journey which took him to Vienna, among other places. Here he made some rather critical entries in his diary about 'Tristan und Isolde'. But on the other hand, we find the following passage in a letter from 22.12.1912 to the director of the Royal Theatre (where he was a conductor 1908—14): "For we still have—or rather do not have, Wagner's 'Tristan', which—along with his 'Meistersinger'—is his most wonderful work and in which the concentrated atmosphere of Romanticism has found its most beautiful expression. (—) I am looking forward immensely to work on this opera and hope that it is true that it is to be produced in May. To all musicians this is perhaps Wagner's finest and strangest work to which they keep returning".[4]

It may appear that there was a kind of ambivalence in Nielsen's attitude to Wagner, but that is probably not the case. It is rather that Nielsen—and with him many other non-German composers of the generation following Wagner's—had to

---

1] Carl Nielsens breve i udvalg ved Irmelin Eggert Møller og Torben Meyer, København 1954, p. 9 (Selected Letters by C. N. edited by I. M. E. and T. M., Copenhagen etc.).
2] The three years older Debussy and the one year younger Satie react in the same way at about the same time.
3] Letters p. 14.
4] Letters, p. 129.

recognize the genius of Wagner, the composer, but could not come to terms with Wagner, the dramatist. The following passage from the 1894 diary seems to me to touch on something important: "The plot must be the 'pole' that goes through a dramatic work; the plot is the trunk, words and sentences are fruits and leaves, but if the trunk is not strong and healthy, it is no use that the fruits look beautiful. (—) Dramas are not made of poetry; it melts." But a critical attitude to Wagner's approach to the musical drama is not enough to solve its problems: How to create a better balance between plot and music; and how to distribute the weight of the drama between the voices and the orchestra. The first of these is the ever returning problem of the dramatic opera and it has been solved in various ways through the ages. The second problem only emerges as a consequence of a number of different solutions of the first.

In the first years of the opera, the problems were not great—not from our point of view, at least—The rôle of the music was secondary; the text was declaimed in a kind of musical recitation. We call it the *recitative*. But it was not long before melodious passages found their way into this recitative, and here the declamation was momentarily replaced by a musically expressive interpretation of a sentence, mostly one with lyrical content. We call it the *arioso*. The next step in the development is that such lyric, dramatically static, passages receive independent status. They become closed musical entities with a structure of their own. Then we have the *aria*. Now the opera is divided into clearly separated 'numbers' connected by recitatives and only the latter serve to carry on the action. During the numbers the action stands still, but to make up for that, the music unfolds in all its beauty borne up by singers of great ability. But the opera as drama has been lost. Plot and text are now only the scaffolding round which the composer builds his music. The opera has become a vocal concerto.

Then a mischievous little brother was born, a lively little fellow who took the audience by storm with his pranks: the comic opera. That, too, had its numbers, but they were short and lively for the comic plots tolerated no delays caused by lengthy arias. This *opera buffa* was written by the same composers who wrote the *opera seria*, so it is not strange that it gave rise to the discussion concerning the relation between action and music. If they wished to approach these two elements more closely to each other than the vocal concerto allowed, there were two ways the composers could go about it: they could make the recitative more like the aria, or the aria could be made more active. Generally speaking, Gluck followed the first of these procedures, whereas Mozart followed the second. Gluck's so-called 'reform' came to influence the serious opera first and most deeply, for its result was obvious to everybody, consisting as it did in an immediately perceptible change in the 'dry' recitative. Mozart's procedure, on the other hand, was more subtle. He kept the dry recitative as a vehicle of the plot, but at the same time he made his music more supple, so that it became possible to move elements from the plot into the closed numbers (arias)—this was not so easily perceived as Gluck's 'reform'. In addition to this, Gluck loudly proclaimed his 'reform' whereas Mozart let his grow quietly and step by step. Finally, Gluck's work belonged in a more elevated sphere: that of the heroic drama, which to his contemporaries was a topic worthy of serious discussion; whereas Mozart continued the lively comic opera, in which the audience in delight (or contempt) did not at once see the new plan behind the smile, nor the way Mozart made his characters more human.

As we have seen, it was Gluck's orchestral accompaniment, his motif—filled recitative which came to exert the greatest influence on the redramatization of the opera. This development necessarily went hand in hand with a change in the text and here the demand for greater literary merit coalesces with the demands of the incipient Romanticism for the unique and the fantastic. National schools saw the light, the old and the new orders clashed, and fruitful interrelations made themselves felt everywhere. The greatest contrasts became juxtaposed. Some replaced the sung recitation by the spoken dialogue ('Fidelio' (1805), 'Der Freischütz' (1821), 'Carmen' (1875)[5], other composers continued along the lines of Gluck's 'reform' towards the through-composed opera ('La Vestale' by Spontini (1807), 'La Muette de Portici' by Auber (1828), 'Boris Godunov' (1874)). And Wagner reaches the 'music drama', where the voice moves between the recitative-like parlando and the sung arioso without perceptible transitions, while the music of the orchestra in a motif-filled texture is the uniting and dramatically active element.

Even after his rejection of Wagner's 'method', Nielsen had many other models to choose from when he was to find a 'pattern' for his first opera. Between the two extremes: the dialogue opera and the through-composed opera there were various possibilities, Verdi's method, for instance. It is not easy to get a clear impression of Nielsen's attitude to Verdi. Judging by his published letters and by what has been published of what he has said and written elsewhere, Verdi did not exist for him. It is possible that the operas from Verdi's second period which were produced in Copenhagen did not attract Nielsen's attention at all, because of their mixture of Italian tradition with dramatic innovations. Verdi always combined his treatment of the fundamental problems with deep reverence for the Italian tradition, and his results may not have appealed to the imagination of his Scandinavian colleague. But it is hardly conceivable that the last two Verdi operas 'Otello'[6] and 'Falstaff'[7] with their far-sighted dramaturgy—so obviously works of genius—should have made no impression on Nielsen, who was always alert to new ideas and who must have taken part in both of them.

The problem concerning the relation between music and plot is solved by Verdi in 'Otello' by an extremely flexible utilization of all the means at his disposal, from the simplest parlando to the fully developed tune in closed form. The repetition of themes always has a dramatic motive; purely abstract patterns are non-existent. The transitions between recitative passages and closed numbers are hardly perceptible; there is nothing left of the 'striking of attitudes' for the closed numbers which we find in the older operas. The music flows in an unbroken stream with more or less emotional charge. No use is made of the decorative function of music but its illustrative and suggestive features are fully developed. The use of the music as a vehicle of the plot (as in Mozart) is only resorted to very occasionally, and then very subtly. Motif migrations between the scenes occur, but only as memory themes, not as 'leitmotifs' in the Wagnerian sense of the word, and therefore not with Wagner's transformation technique. The problem concerning the distribution of the weight of the drama between voices and orchestra was not urgent to the Italian. With his great reverence for the tradition of the Italian opera, it was a matter of course to him that the drama was to be

---

5] The sung recitatives as we know them in 'Carmen' are not Bizet's, they were composed by Ernest Guiraud for the Vienna performance.
6] First produced in Copenhagen on 20.4.1898.
7] First produced in Copenhagen on 16.1.1895.

carried by the voices, to which the orchestra had to subject itself. But in the later stages of his development the orchestra leaves its accompanying or merely atmosphere creating rôle to take its place among the dramatis personae. Thus it helps to keep the pace where the drama will not tolerate delay caused by the vocal cantilene.

Carl Nielsen found the subject matter for his first opera in the Old Testament story of Saul, the king of Israel, and the conflicts between him and David, his successor. The dramatic remodelling of the subject matter as found in the Books of Samuel, Nielsen left to the playwright Einar Christiansen, who had performed similar work for other Danish composers. Christiansen constructed the following plot:

Act I. In Saul's House in Gilgal.[8]
(1) The Israelites have awaited Samuel's arrival in vain for seven days, for before they can take the field against the invading Philistines the prophet must offer to the Lord the sacrifice of the people. Now King Saul makes a sudden decision: he himself will sacrifice to the Lord. His son Jonathan is shocked at this sacrilege and implores his father to wait for the prophet. However, Saul's patience is at an end. Must he, the Lord's anointed, be kept waiting by Samuel? (2) But when the smoke from the burnt offering and the song of the people rise towards the sky, Samuel appears among them and proclaims the anger of the Lord at the breach of his commandment: the kingdom is to be torn out of Saul's hand and given to the man after the Lord's own heart. And an evil spirit is to enter Saul and be like drought and fire. The prophet turns his back on the disobedient Saul and leaves. (3) Horror-stricken all depart from the King, whom the Lord has rejected, only his son remains with him. But Saul will not listen to Jonathan's advice to try to be reconciled with the Lord through repentance. (4) In haughty defiance he rises against Jehovah, whose creature he is. But the thought of the angel of death breaks his pride. Disheartened and broken he sits on his throne. (5) Suddenly he hears singing. Jonathan has fetched his friend David, the shepherd, who can play the harp and sing so beautifully. He has often helped Jonathan through periods of despair and now he succeeds in loosening the knots in Saul's spirit so that he gets courage to take the field at the head of his army. With his son he marches on the Philistines while David, now one of the king's servants, remains behind. (6) But he is not alone. Enraptured by his song, the king's daughter, Michal, approaches and the two are alone in the hall. David has seen the king's daughter once before and since that time he has often thought of her beauty. She too has noticed the handsome shepherd, and soon they have declared their love for each other.
Act II. In Saul's House in Gilgal.
(1) While David is singing to Saul a messenger arrives with tidings that the army of the Philistines has returned after its defeat. At its head goes the giant Goliath, who disdainfully challenges Israel's best man to single combat. The king hesitates, remembering Samuel's curse. David steps forward. He has often fought against lions and bears to protect his flock; now he wants to fight Goliath. He refuses helmet and shield and he wants no sword. With a sling as his only weapon he wants to meet the Philistine. The king promises him Michal if he is victorious, and confident in the Lord's favour, David goes to the unequal fight. (2) Proud but afraid Michal is waiting among her handmaidens for news of David. (3) Jonathan brings it to her: Goliath has been killed! (4) The people rejoice as Saul announces

8] There is no division of the acts into scenes in the piano score, it has been made by the author of this article.

the double cause of celebration: the victory and the nuptials of David and Michal. (5) Singing and dancing the people hail their hero: "Saul hath slain his thousands, and David his ten thousands." This rouses Saul's anger and he bids them be silent, giving as his reason that he is troubled by a pain in his head. Jonathan turns to David for help and at once David takes his harp. He sings in praise of the Lord and swears allegiance to Him, but Saul calls him a hypocrite and in a violent fit of passion seeks to kill him with his javelin. The nimble youth escapes being hit by the murderous weapon and flees with the words: "Vengeance is mine saith the Lord. We shall meet again, King Saul!"

Act III. Saul's Camp in the Wilderness of Ziph.

(1) In the moonlight Michal and Jonathan sit gazing at the stars in the sky. Her troubled thoughts are with David, who has taken refuge in the wilderness. (2) When they have lain down to sleep, David and Abishai, his companion, appear on the rocks above the camp. They descend and stand looking at Saul in his troubled sleep. Abishai offers to kill him, but David prevents him from taking the life of the Lord's anointed, and bids him take the king's spear and cruse of water. Silently they depart with these things, but (3) from the rocks David awakens the sleepers with shouts. Saul at once recognizes David's voice; moved by his loyalty he offers him peace and calls him down. In the light of the rising sun the people sing about the pact which has been concluded between their king and their hero. (4) From the rocks Abishai has seen a caravan approaching. It is Samuel carried by his servants, blind, ill and full of days. (5) The Lord has commanded him to anoint David as the King of Israel. Saul protests: has Israel not a king? But Samuel answers him that the Lord has long grieved over him and that soon his rule will be at an end. When the prophet has fulfilled his duty, he implores the Lord to take his soul, his prayer is granted and he expires in David's arms. (6) Saul furiously orders David to be seized, but Michal intervenes and warns them against laying violent hands on the Lord's anointed. Again David has to take flight, but this time Michal goes with him—nobody dares to stop them.

Act IV, part 1. In the Witch's House in Endor.

(1) One stormy night Saul disguises himself and goes to the witch in Endor and asks her to conjure up Samuel's spirit. Full of fear—for Saul has forbidden the practice of witchcraft—but tempted by Saul's gold and promises, she does as he wants. But when Samuel emerges from the darkness of the grave, he has no good news for Saul: at dawn the Philistines will sack his camp and he and his sons are to die.

Act IV, part 2. On Mount Gilboa.

(2) Jonathan has been mortally wounded during the battle with the Philistines and has fled up the mountain together with Abner, and here he falls down; dying he pays homage for the last time to David, the deliverer. (3) Now Saul appears on the scene, wounded and exhausted. At the sight of his son's dead body he despairs and orders Abner to stab him. Abner, however, does not dare to lay violent hands on his king. Then Saul stretches his sword towards the sky in defiance of the Lord, and blaming Him for his own guilt, he kills himself. (4) While David is mourning beside Jonathan's dead body, the people hail their new king.

There is no lack of plot and action in this tale and thus Nielsen got his 'pole'. It is also rich in dramatic incident, but we feel the lack of something to keep us in suspense from beginning to end. In the tale itself there is an element which is more epic than dramatic: the prophecy of Saul's downfall is repeated three times (I,2; III,5; IV,1), and the first of these prophecies comes so soon after the beginning of the opera that Saul's fate is clear even before David appears. The outcome of the struggle for power has thus been known from the beginning

80

A family circle. From the left: Hans Borge, Anne Marie (Telmanyi), Carl Nielsen, Irmelin (Eggert Moller), Mrs Carl Nielsen.

"Saul og David." I. act: David sings before Saul. From the left: Saul (Niels Juel Simonsen), Jonathan (Peter Cornelius), David (Vilhelm Herold), Michal (Emilie Ulrich).

and nothing depends on the efforts of the two parties. We are reminded of the old *deus ex machina* technique, which was never beneficial to the drama.

But then it can be said that the opera is not about the struggle for power between Saul and David, but about Saul's struggle with his God. Here too, however, a non-dramatic element creeps in, as Saul is deprived of his free will when an evil spirit enters him (I. Samuel 16,14-16; in the opera: I,2) Can we, then, take Saul's defiance of God seriously? Is it psychologically interesting?

If, before he set to work, Nielsen had consulted those before him who had made use of the same subject matter in operas; he would have been told that none of them had had any lasting success. His greatest predecessor in Denmark, J. P. E. Hartmann, who had tried his hand at the same story in collaboration with Hans Andersen, might have been able to give him some good advice. But the self-willed young Carl Nielsen would hardly have taken any advice to the effect that he ought to stop working at the heavily encumbered subject. "This great and strange subject stirred and haunted me, so that for long periods I could not free myself of it no matter where I was—even when I was sitting in the orchestra with my second violin, busy with ballets and vaudevilles."[9]

The composer's obsession with the subject matter together with the skilful arrangement of the scenes on the part of the librettist went a long way towards weighing up the dramatic weaknesses. The sharp delineation of character and the clear contrast between the brief incidents supplied the composer with an excellent framework.

There is no overture.—Nielsen did the right thing in confronting the audience with Saul straight away. In a short introduction from the orchestra we are given the themes which throughout the scene serve to illustrate Saul's impatience, and he has been given the first line: "Is he coming? Is the prophet coming?" When he decides to sacrifice, a maestoso theme depicts the resolute king (piano score p. 11, system 1, bar 1) and we hear the same theme when in spite of Jonathan's warning he begins the sacrifice (16,3,1). During the sacrifice itself, the second half of this theme has a combining function. When Samuel interrupts him, Saul's agitated state of mind is contrasted with Samuel's heavily striding themes which are attached to a fixed formula when we come to the prophecy (30,4,3). The rhythmic character of this formula was also used to prepare us for Samuel's appearance and it is followed up all through the dialogue.

Immediately after Samuel has left the stage we get the first impression of Saul as possessed by the evil spirit. His mood changes abruptly from the deepest despondency—"The Lord does not know me"—to the fiercest defiance—"let the people die out"—after which he relapses into brooding silence. Alone on the stage—after Jonathan has hurried away to fetch David—Saul has his monologue to Jehovah: "If I could rise against thee, thou King of Kings!" This monologue, both as to its kind and form inspired by Verdi's monologues, is the first climax

---

9] "Politiken" 27.2.1929.

of the opera. Its similarity with Iago's monologue ('Otello' Act II) is so striking
that both the librettist and the composer must have been directly inspired by
this. Iago says: "I believe in a merciless God who created me in his image."
Saul says: "The Lord is evil! And I myself am evil. For evil has he created me."
Both monologues have a theme-carrying orchestral accompaniment under a
vocal recitative, and both are in closed form. But naturally Nielsen did not copy
Saul's monologue directly from Iago's—he could not have done that, for the two
characters are totally different. Iago is quite firm in his belief in evil. He is a
fearless mocker, even of death. Saul is not essentially evil; his is a divided soul,
and he fears death. Therefore the two monologues develop in different ways.
Iago's is economically built up on two themes which alternate in supple combination with the text. Saul's monologue is a closed sequence (ABCA₁) which sinks
back where it began. The first section (39,2,1) gradually builds up the tension,
it is brooding, carried by dull orchestral themes. The second section depicts the
flaming defiance (40,1,2). At the beginning it is dominated by the voice, but
towards the end the orchestra picks up the defiance theme from the previous
scene (36,1,1) (here is a similarity with Iago's monologue, which also takes one
of its motifs from a previous scene), develops it into falling triplets which in
a diminuendo lead on to the third section; this gives itself up to fear of death.
Here (42,2,2), in a slower tempo, the voice leads in an expressive arioso (notice
the chromatically gliding harmony; this is found again in the scene where the
dejected Saul refuses to take up Goliath's challenge). Finally, in voice as well as
orchestra, the fourth section (43,2,3) relaxes the tension that was built up in the
first section, of which it is a shortened repetition. Nielsen's monologue and that
of Verdi are equally satisfactory as to form, each in its own place.

A new side of Saul's character unfolds itself during the feast celebrating David's victory over Goliath. The desire for power breeds jealousy: he suspects David
of being the successor to his throne foretold by Samuel. At first — pianissimo in the
violas (129,1,1) — we hear the motif from the first defiance scene (36,1,1). In
spite of the pianissimo this motif strikes the ear because of its D natural — the
minor seventh in an E major chord with a major seventh (D sharp). A new motif,
simple, pastoral, is introduced by the oboe in the following short orchestral interlude (130,2,2). On presentation it looks as follows:

Ex. 1

While Saul's jealousy is mounting, it undergoes a number of changes, or more
correctly, distortions, mainly in the bass and finally reaches the motif to which
Saul throws his javelin at David. As the motif in its first form undoubtedly
describes David as the 'shepherd of the brook' (to this text we hear it 132,1,1), its

transformations symbolize Saul's distorted picture of David. This is one of the few Wagnerian touches in 'Saul og David'.

The strongest swing in the opposite direction is seen in the reconciliation scene (III,3). At this point, when Saul embraces David, the oboe theme from the prelude to the second act is quoted. This prelude to what may be called the 'David act' describes the two different sides of David—the warrior and the singer. The oboe theme is the singer's theme—and by using this theme Saul expresses how sincerely he wishes to be reconciled, bearing in mind that it was as a singer that David came to be so close to him. This is one of the few examples of a psychologically used motif.

In the final scenes it is as if the Saul figure dissolves. In the witch-of-Endor-scene (IV,1) the music centres on the situation whereas Saul is treated purely melodramatically. And in spite of the fact that IV,3 begs recalls to earlier scenes, Nielsen, perhaps intentionally, omits them: at that particular moment Saul is without past, without future. His mourning song over Jonathan's dead body is a short arioso passage; the last time that he turns to Jehovah before he falls on his sword he does so in a recitative passage held together by the orchestra's development motif.

The David figure has three facets: singer, warrior, lover. The librettist has tried to overcome the difficulties which arise in an opera from having to set the singer apart from the others, by letting David speak in rhymed verse in this capacity. Nielsen followed his librettist by giving his songs a hymnal character.

It is in his capacity of singer that David enters Saul's house, and it is in this scene (I,5) that the singer has a dramatic function. This accounts for the length of the scene and its richness in musical content. It falls into three sections: in the first David presents himself to Saul (44,4,3). It is introduced by an oboe theme of the sort that is so often associated with David (cp. 130,2,2; ex. 1) and which by their pastoral character describe him as the shepherd. After attracting Saul's attention by means of this introductory stanza he turns directly to the king in the second passage with a comforting song (46,3,1). This raises Saul's spirits (the first motif from the defiance monologue (39,2,2) is heard brighten from E minor to C major (47,4,1-2)). In the third passage David praises the Lord. Before this otherwise independent F major passage is completed, the final part of the oboe theme from the first section returns (53,4,2) and formally rounds off the whole.

David's second song (II,1) is only a fragment. As a direct continuation of the prelude it completes the picture of David and furnishes a connection to the preceding song through references to the first song's third section.

As in the third section of the first song and in the fragmentary second song, David addresses the Lord in his third song (II,5). This is in the spirit of the Biblical Psalms of David and like these it is accompanied by the singer on his harp.[10] This song is that which perhaps most closely resembles an aria melody

10] The Biblical harp—kinnor—known now as a lyre, is akin to the Greek kithara. This was only used for gay songs and characterizes the Biblical David as the gay singer.

[11], but it has not the form of an aria, perhaps because it is a fragment: Saul interrupts David before he can return to the song's main key (G flat major).

David, the singer, now disappears from the scene, where he has not left any great impression. The same may be said of David, the warrior, in so far as we have only seen him indirectly. We see him for the first time in I,5, where a short motif, one of the war motifs (58,4,1), is heard to the words "but is a hero and a warrior to boot". Stronger and clearer, but also only indirectly, David, the hero, is described in the first section of the rightly famous prelude to the second act, where the warlike features (heralded by trumpet dissonances) match well with the hymnal tone at the end of the section. When after that, David steps forward offering to take up Goliath's challenge (II,1), the trumpets sound the following motif[12] (86,2,1):

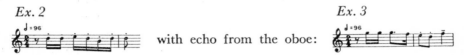

Ex. 2 with echo from the oboe: *Ex. 3*

which goes through the whole scene. The motif-form and the choice of the oboe (shawm) as the shepherd's instrument—its sound may be said to be like that of a miniature trumpet—is an apt characterization of the sling-armed shepherd-warrior.

Jonathan's account of the fight adds nothing new to the indirect picture. However, the scene where David descends into Saul's camp shows him, if not as a warrior, then as a man of great courage. The music to this scene does not contribute to the delineation of David's character, it is decorative and highly suggestive.

Only one scene is devoted to the characterization of David, the lover, but to make up for that, its treatment of this side of David is exhaustive, and at the same time this scene is the second musical climax of the opera: it is the love duet which ends the first act.

The framework of this duet is one of the most perfect examples of the dramatic sense of Nielsen even when he is in his most lyrical mood. With great sensitivity he pictures the two young people's situation as described by his librettist, who had quoted from the Song of Solomon, this collection of ancient Semitic nuptial and love songs in which the lovers alternately sing praise to the beauty and grace of each other's body.

David begins the duet cautiously, rather shyly, pausing frequently, with a semi-recitative stanza, the orchestra accompanying with the clarinet as the leading instrument in the first motif of the duet.

11] Note also the way time is gained at the end of the text by the use of the empty word "ja...".

12] The motif is derived from a passage in the duet (I,6), where it says, "Proud as he stood beneath the banner facing the enemy from Gath"—here too with an echo from the oboe (65,3,1).

84

Imperceptibly the oboe continues directly into another motif:

Ex. 5

This motif, which is capable of further development, is slowly modulated by the orchestra while David in an arioso without a definite motif confides his longing to Michal. This introductory section (andantino amoroso) is replaced by a livelier tempo (agitato) when Michal starts to sing, and the opening's soft, dark A flat major is transformed into a light D major with the voice leading in a melody which betrays Saul's temperamental daughter.[13]

The third section (E flat major, tempo primo) stems from the second motif of the first section (ex. 5) and here it is taken over for the first time by the voice, but only by David's, even though the section otherwise presents a speedier change of voices as a sign of the lovers' growing intimacy and eagerness. The fourth section unwinds with breathless haste in erotic incitement (A flat major/ F major/ A flat major, allegro con fuoco). In the fifth section (A flat major, tempo primo) they plight their troth. It is connected textually with the preceding section, and with the first section with regard to motif. Here for the first time Michal takes over David's motif (ex. 5). In the following orchestral epilogue we hear both of the opening themes in close sequence.

The contents of the duet can be summarized in the following schematic arrangement, where a and b indicate the two opening themes (exx. 4 and 5) while x and y indicate non-recurring themes:

A (a + b)-B(x)-C(b)-D(y)-E(b)-epilogue (a + b).

Even though the duet continues progressively, and even though the expressiveness of the sections shifts continually from the told to the dreamt and from the dreamt to the ecstatic, in spite of this, Nielsen has managed to place the shifting scenes on a firm musical basis which reminds one very much of the rondo form. The duet is one of the places in 'Saul og David' where the two basic problems have

13] E.g. with a predilection for sudden movement from height to depth, often with interrupted tones (see e.g. 64,4,2; 90,4,2; 97,1,4; 98,2,1; 113,3,2).

found their most satisfying solution through the closest possible connection between plot and music and through the ideal interaction between voice and orchestra.

Michal has revealed the essential sides of her temperament in this duet. Justifiably she borrows her words from Shulamite of the Song of Solomon, both of them being upright and open in their warm sensuality. This and other sides of her nature are also revealed in her scene with the handmaidens (II,2), where she sways between pride in her lover's courage and despair caused by the thought of his possible defeat[14]. The scene is divided into three parts; they are bound together partly by a striking orchestral motif (99,2,5) and partly by an often repeated choral refrain (99,4,2). With immense speed the scene carries through to Jonathan's arrival with news of victory, already guessed, which leads to a return to the light tone of the opening.

The duet which opens the third act does not add anything to the delineation of Michal's character. It creates an atmosphere and, while it is superfluous to the plot, it is a lyrical resting point, a nocturne.[15]

But Nielsen has filled this night scene with wonderful music in an extremely ingenious form which—with only one contrast—blends the themes together in such a way that the music can follow the text and yet create a self-contained, thoroughly satisfying form in itself. It is the prelude which before the curtain rises presents the essentials of the two main parts of the tripartite form. After a five bar opening we hear a motif (a) first presented by the cor anglais, then by the flute. This motif is continued each time in a new way (x,y). When the curtain rises the first phrase is Jonathan's with a motif (b_1) which Michal takes up as her phrase (b_2). But the intensity of her feelings is so great that the phrase must be expanded; this occurs on the a-motif, but with a new continuation (z), which is carried on by Jonathan. Michal rises and asks anxiously: "Where walketh now my lover?" Her uneasiness expresses itself in a short tripartite allegro. Jonathan replies reassuringly: "He looketh at the same stars as we do"; simultaneously the orchestra returns to the opening with a part of the prelude, now with the harmony of the voices added. The ingeniously flexible and yet firmly woven pattern looks as follows in schematic form:

$$\text{Opening—A}(ax\text{-}ay\text{-}b_1\text{-}b_2\text{-}az)\text{—B}(d\text{-}e\text{-}d)\text{—A}(ay)$$

It may be said that the opera deals more with Saul than with David. It is first and foremost Saul's reactions which determine the course of events. Generally, his reactions are described shortly and sharply—with the exception of the defiance monologue (I,4)—whilst the results of his reactions are awarded a greater part of

---

14] It must be admitted that David's departure is rather abrupt (97,4,2-3) (two bars!) and does not match the heartfelt tone of the love duet.

15] This implies no criticism! The creation of atmosphere in lyrical passages, with the voices carrying the music, has its legitimate place in the opera as a vocal work of art. It becomes a problem only when timing is disturbed or its sole function is to provide scope for the singers.

the work and as such must carry the musical weight. The following survey will illustrate this (italics denote great musical weight):

I. Saul's disobedience—*The Sacrifice*—(1st prophecy)—*Saul's defiance—David's first song*—Saul's pleasure—*The love duet*.

II. Saul's despondency—*Michal's scene with her handmaidens—The Hallelujah chorus*—Saul's pleasure—*The reunion chorus and feast scene*—Saul's anger—*David's third song*—Saul's anger and David's flight.

III. Saul's anger—*The covenant song*—(2nd prophecy)—Saul's anger.

IV, part 1. Saul's irresolution—(3rd prophecy)

IV, part 2. Saul's defeat and death—*David's complaint and the ovation of the people*.

Among the closed numbers only the nocturne (III,1) is right outside the plot (but it is a beautiful enrichment of the otherwise meagre third act). As previously mentioned, the music creates the atmosphere and is an example of Nielsen's use of its suggestive power. But we feel its suggestive function even stronger in the witch-of-Endor-scene (IV,1). At this point it is typical of Nielsen not to resort to tone effects: he gives us a very simple imitative melodious movement for two solo violas. These instruments do not illustrate anything and they are not associated with any particular phenomenon; but their sonorous alto pitch is very useful in creating a sinister atmosphere.

There are, however, several places in the opera where the illustrative function of the instruments is tied up with the character of the music and as such leads the audience in the desired direction. The association of the oboe with David has already been mentioned, together with its use as a trumpet echo, where these martial-sounding instruments are used to characterize the warrior. But they are also used, alone or together with the trombones, to illustrate war (e.g. 233,1,2 and 255,3,3). In general we can say that the orchestral movement is pierced with moments which can, and perhaps ought to, be interpreted as being illustrative (a sure example is 116,2,1, where the path of the stone from David's sling is shown figuratively).

All these are, however, no more than isolated features. But in 'Saul og David' there is also one long orchestral piece where music is purely illustrative. We are here thinking of the 'war music', which is played before closed curtains between IV, part 1 and IV, part 2. Such scene-connecting interludes during changes of set are quite common, but what is special here is that the interlude describes action (the fight), and that the chorus helps to make it more concrete. Nielsen may have learnt such a use of the interlude from Wagner[16], less likely from Verdi[17]. As a rule such illustrating interludes before closed curtains have the

---

16] An example is the richly illustrative interlude which in 'Rheingold' connects the second and the third scenes and which describes Wotan's and Loge's journey to Nibelheim.

17] In 'La Forza del Destino' there is an exact parallel in the interlude between III,1 and III,2 (turmoil), but in the first place this opera was not performed in Copenhagen until 1937 and in the second place this change of scene has disappeared during one of the many adaptions this opera has been subjected to.

effect of tricks, and the interlude in 'Saul og David' cannot be said to be altogether without this effect. Incidentally, the impact of the voices in the last part of the interlude is probably weaker than intended for the text is difficult to hear through the curtain.

On the other hand, the dramatic employment of the choruses is wholly admirable. They are never merely decorative, but always have a function in the development of the plot, and musically they include some of the most beautiful passages of the opera, especially the chorus in III,3, where the pact between Saul and David is concluded. It is composed in a fugal texture for fourpart chorus and five solo voices. It is true that it brings the action to a complete standstill, but at a natural point: just before Samuel's arrival, when it gathers speed again; and so this chorus with its magnificent music has the effect of relieving the tension. In general, it can be established that it is not—as has been maintained—the choruses which encumber the opera and make it oratorical. The encumbrance is in the tale itself, its kind and subject matter. But actually it is not heavier than that of many other serious operas whose musical qualities cause us to make allowances for their dramatic weaknesses. Such qualities are also present in 'Saul og David', and they are strong enough to ensure the opera a long life.

"Sometimes I feel that I am not myself—Carl August Nielsen—but a kind of hollow pipe through which flows a stream of music moved by gentle but strong powers in continuous blissful vibrations. At such times it is pure bliss to be a musician, believe me."[18] In such a happy frame of mind Carl Nielsen set to work on the comic opera 'Maskarade'. He had taken the subject matter from Holberg's identically named comedy (1724) and he left the writing of the libretto to Vilhelm Andersen, the literary historian. There could be no question of taking over the text and plot of the comedy directly; it had to be adapted. The first act of the opera is thus a concentration of the most important scenes from Holberg's first and second acts; then follows the scene in the street, which is of the librettist's own invention (the second act of the opera) and finally a transformation of the intermezzo between the first and second acts of the comedy into a lengthy divertissement with occasional bursts of action which contribute to the *dénouement*.

This gives rise to considerable changes in the delineation of character. Leonora, whom Holberg gave a short but not insignificant scene (III,1 in the comedy) becomes a somewhat pale character. But that is of less consequence than the changes in the two fathers in the play. In the comedy Jeronimus is an extremely dignified and conservative old gentleman and Leonard is a no less dignified advocate of modern liberalism (though eventually (in III,4) he is forced to admit

---

18] Letter from 18.2.1905; Letters p. 68.

88

that he was mistaken on this point). He is shown as the more sensitive of the two, a warm-hearted father caught between his feelings for his daughter and the duties of convention.

In the opera both these characters have undergone a change in the direction of the farcical. Jeronimus allows himself to be made drunk and become a laughing stock at the masquerade; Leonard becomes a foolish and amorous provincial who wants to make use of his visit to town to sow some wild oats left over from his youth. The coarsening of the characters and the lengthy divertissement damages the third act so that we lose interest in the *dénouement*, which is also musically somewhat pointless. It is fairly evident that these shortcomings would not have been remedied by Nielsen's unrealized plan "of providing a bandage in the shape of an orchestral interlude"[19] to bridge the gap between the second and third acts.

But the delineation of character is not the opera's strong point. Nielsen himself stressed that he had been attracted mainly by the intermezzo and by the masquerade features[20]. This means that from the beginning he was more interested in situation-comedy than in character drama. Here he is at one with the tradition of the opera buffa.

In its original form the Italian opera buffa is closely associated with the masque, the commedia dell'arte, whose stock masks it took over. Its main feature was grotesque farce. On the other hand, it had a certain naive realism and a keen eye for human weaknesses, which it emphasized in order to caricature them, for in contradistinction to the opera seria, the opera buffa at once became entertainment for the masses and musically too it bore a clearly popular stamp. It is true that in the course of its development there were repeated efforts to introduce some refinement, but its typical situations: slapstick—duels—drunkenness—disguise and mistaken identity—remained integral parts of it; and the break of illusion which consisted in the actors addressing the audience across the footlights also lived on even in the highest form of the musical comedy.[21] The lovers constitute a new feature: they are taken more or less seriously, and their musical portrayal brings in elements from the opera seria. About the middle of the 18th century the opera buffa shows an increasingly marked tendency to approach the sentimental domestic comedy. This means that the opera seria da capo aria with its coloraturas gains a foothold in the buffa, but it does not cause the disappearance of characteristic forms in the buffa, for instance the strophic song, the bipartite cavatina, the rondo and several other complex forms. Flexibility is still demanded of the buffa composers and they seek to meet this demand by introducing forms with increasing pitch in which the action goes hand in hand with the music, to illustrate the mounting tension at the ends of acts. These various action-furthering finale forms are the most important contribution of the opera buffa to the development of the musical drama. With regard to this kind of finale writing Mozart is pre-eminent.

We see a parallel development in the French opéra comique, but as its starting point is altogether different from that of the opera buffa, the results of this development—up to a certain point—are different too. The opéra comique grew naturally out of the vaudeville, which was a comedy with inset songs, and it was faithful to its origin in so far as the spoken

19] Cp. the programme of the Royal Theatre of 25.11.1925.
20] Cp. 'Politiken' 15.10.1905.
21] E.g. in Figaro's "Aprite un po' quegli occhi" (Ye men, be not blind).

dialogue remained a characteristic feature.[22] Nor was the comic element so dominating as in the early opera buffa and it was not so closely associated with definite scenes. Right from the beginning it was written in collaboration with librettists of literary ambition, mostly it dealt realistically with everyday middle-class life and often it led up to a moral which was declaimed at the end by the whole company[23]. Its songs: ariettas—romanzas—chansons—were all of a popular kind, like the songs of the vaudevilles, which were on everybody's lips, and their origin in the dancing song (gavotte and menuet) was frequently obvious. Besides we often find epic songs (ballades) and decorative choruses of peasants, huntsmen and soldiers in the opéra comique, even ballet may be met with. In variety of forms it is not behind the Italian opera buffa: there are both the simple strophic song, the typical French rondeau (with minor-key darkening in the middle) and the da capo aria. Typically French features in the instrumental forms include the programme-overture (with presentation of themes from the opera itself) and the entr'acte music. The French opéra comique came to exert considerable influence on the romantic opera through its great flexibility and variety and not least its 'realism' and the great care taken over the declamation—characteristics not typical of the opera buffa.

But in this sphere, too, romanticism heralds a mixture of *genres*. The tendency—present already in the opera buffa—to take some of the characters more seriously, while others—mostly servants—remain purely comic, gains ground so that sentimental, heroic or adventurous elements come to be the principal themes, whereas comic and laughter-provoking elements are reduced to the function of commenting on the main action[24]. Only the Italians hold their own for some time against the sentimental tendencies of the time and this is principally due to Rossini's clear and witty handling of the unadulterated situation-comedy. The last example of the old buffo art is found in 'Don Pasquale' (1843) by Donizetti, who could deliver works in all *genres*: the romantic tragedy ('Lucia di Lammermoor'), the lyrical comedy ('L'Elisir d'Amore'), the French opéra comique ('La Fille du Régiment'). But that was the end. The sentimental art of the romantic period had no use for the old buffo pranks; the musical comedy is now presented in national colours with gravity underneath the lyrical surface ('The Bartered Bride') and even with a good deal of propaganda ('Die Meistersinger'). Not until half a century after Donizetti does anyone dare to look at the world in a humorous light and now Verdi raises the comic opera to a level of artistry so subtle that his work is miles above the heads of the audience, who in 'Falstaff' (1893) cannot recognize the features of his buffo predecessors.

In 1905 Carl Nielsen sets to work on 'Maskarade' and in the intoxication of creative activity he rattles off musical pranks on his music paper. While he was at work he was hardly conscious of taking part in an anti-romantic reaction, of being—in other words—modern. He probably just enjoyed letting himself go after the heavy work exacted by 'Saul og David'[25]. However, looking back to-day, we see that in the very choice of the subject matter there is a tendency which

---

22] So characteristic that the opéra comique becomes a kind of *genre* name which is also used for works which are definitely not comic. Dialogue operas like 'Fidelio' and 'Carmen' (in its original version) are thus called "opéra comique".

23] The finale in Mozart's 'Die Entführung aus dem Serail' is a typical opéra comique finale and there are also traces of the opéra comique in 'Don Giovanni', which—as is often overlooked—is a 'dramma giocoso', a gay drama.

24] This development had been completed in 'Die Zauberflöte' by Mozart, which contains all the ingredients mentioned above. At the same time, this opera is typical of the mixture of musical style levels and we find in it practically all forms: from the opera seria (The Queen of Night) to the popular vaudeville (Papageno).

25] In 1922 we see the same when immediately after the great Fifth Symphony he goes on to write the Wind Quintet.

90

in its deliberate unpretentiousness heralds a new epoch. And as is so often the case with new tendencies, they date from a time before the immediately preceding generations.

Bearing in mind Nielsen's great love of Mozart,[26] one would perhaps tend to ascribe to this unsurpassed master of the music comedy a very great influence on 'Maskarade'. But in fact, there are very few Mozartian features in Nielsen's opera, the reason being that he takes his starting point in the masque rather than in the character play. It was not possible for Nielsen to follow Mozart's psychological delineation of character. We need only think of the two servants, who in both operas are all-important for the development of the plot: Figaro and Henrik, and we see at once that already in the libretto there is a world of difference between the versatile servant in 'Le Nozze di Figaro' and the liveried jester in 'Maskarade'. True, there is something of a rebel in them both, but it is also true that here the difference between them is most striking; in 'Le Nozze di Figaro' it is a motif which contributes to keep the action moving and it determines Figaro's whole attitude to the count. In 'Maskarade' it is of secondary importance and by no means the only thing which makes Henrik side with his master against the older generation. But then, we must not forget that Beaumarchais' Figaro is 54 years younger than Holberg's Henrik and that 'Le Mariage de Figaro' (1778) is a comedy with a more pronounced social tendency than Holberg's gaily satirical 'Mascarade' (1724).

The plot as adapted by Vilhelm Andersen looks as follows:

Act I. In a Room in Jeronimus' House. In the Spring of 1723.

(1) Jeronimus' son, Leander, has been to a masquerade with Henrik, his valet, so it is far into the afternoon when Leander finally wakes up. It is even more difficult for Henrik to wake up properly. Leander must slap his face before he realizes that he is no longer at the masquerade. However, his spirits rise when he is informed by his master that they are going again that same evening. The reason is that Leander has met a lovely girl there with whom he has fallen violently in love. But unfortunately there is a snag: his father has already promised that he is to marry Mr Leonard's daughter (whom he has never seen) and Henrik must explain to his master that breach of promise is a serious matter, which will get him into trouble with his father, his future father-in-law and even with the authorities. Leander, who is rapt in thoughts of his beloved only listens with one ear to what Henrik has to say; but on one point they agree: they must go to the masquerade again, for Henrik too has fish to fry there. (2) Now they are interrupted by Leander's mother, the handsome Mrs Magdelone, a woman in her prime and not at all averse to a bit of dancing. She really is a good dancer, which is shown in the sample of her art she delights the two young men with. (3) Unfortunately this is brought to an abrupt end when the master of the house suddenly enters the room in an angry mood and bids them be silent. Worse is to follow: he knows that they intend to go to the masquerade, but he will prevent that by simply locking them up and placing a guard at the entrance of the house. Nor is he softened when he learns that Leander has failed to keep an appointment: he has not been to Mr Leonard's to propose, and to make matters even worse he has fallen in love with an unknown Miss at the masquerade. Furiously

---

26] His admiration of Mozart is seen in e.g. 'Mozart og vor Tid' (M. and our Time) in 'Tilskueren' (a periodical) (1906), reprinted in 'Levende Musik' (Living Music).

Jeronimus packs the two rascals out of the room and (4) curses the masquerades, which have turned the whole town upside-down and now threaten to ruin his own good name. (5) Henrik announces Mr Leonard's arrival. This dapper elderly gentleman seems to be somewhat worried, and it proves that their problems are identical; it turns out that his daughter is rebelling against his plans for her future. The two disappointed fathers, then, are in the same position and have no reason to reproach each other, but together they can plot to prevent a scandal. (6) To that end Mr Jeronimus calls Arv, one of this servants, and instructs him to keep watch outside the house that same night. Then he calls Leander and Henrik in order that they may give an explanation of their shameful behaviour before Mr Leonard. Henrik is the better talker, so from him these old gentlemen learn that the country were not fit to live in if you could not have a fling now and then. His defence of the masquerade is so spirited that he half convinces Mr Leonard, but as a respectable citizen he still has some misgivings about these functions to which everybody has access, even servants like Henrik. But the latter is ready with his answer: in the first place it is an advantage to the master that his servant does not stand outside in all kinds of weather and catches cold so that he cannot do his work, in the second place the poor also ought to have a glimpse of the joys and pleasures of life. But Jeronimus abruptly makes an and of all this foolish talk and demands that the two sinners offer Mr Leonard an apology. They have nearly finished this—from dictation—but when they are told to wind it up with a solemn promise that Leander will marry Mr Leonard's daughter, their submission is at an end and a violent quarrel ensues.

Act II. In the Street. (On the left the brightly illuminated play-house; on the right Mr Jeronimus' house, dark and gloomy).

(1) The watchman is walking through the streets announcing that the clock has struck eight. Arv, who is a superstitious boy from the country, is not happy about his watch. He sings a hymn to fortify himself, but unluckily it is about being at peace with one's conscience and Arv's is not as clear as it ought to be. Then he comforts himself with some food and after that he sings a song. (2) But there is something wrong with that too, for suddenly a ghost appears and announces to the horrified Arv that he is soon to die. It would be better for him if he confessed his sins at once. Now Arv has to clear his conscience of all the petty thefts he has been guilty of: a little flour, a little wine, a little bread, a little meat. That must be enough to avoid going to hell, or so he thinks. But the ghost shows no mercy and so Arv must confess that he has stolen cook's virginity too. Now Henrik—for the ghost is he—cannot contain his laughter any longer. Arv is indignant, but he is also at the mercy of Henrik, who knows far too much by now, and he must pay for his discretion by letting him and Leander pass. (3) The street begins to fill with people of many sorts on their way to the masquerade. Just as Henrik and Leander are about to enter the play-house there arrives a sedan-chair with two masked ladies. They are Leander's beloved and her maid. Leander and his beloved greet each other in transports of joy and their love nearly bursts into flames while the more prosaic servants watch them ironically. A noise from Mr Jeronimus' house makes them retreat into the play-house. (5) The noise was made by Mr Jeronimus himself; he has found out that the birds have flown, but he knows where to look for them. However, before he can enter the play-house he must disguise himself and put on a mask and he goes to the mask shop with Arv. (6) Now it is Mrs Magdelone's turn to tiptoe across the street. Here she meets Mr Leonard, but as they are both wearing masks they do not recognize each other and agree to go to the masquerade together. (7) Dressed as Bacchus and Cupid respectively, Jeronimus and Arv are now ready to launch their attack on the masquerade and all its evils. (8) While the watchman announces the stroke of nine to the accompaniment of the dance-music from the play-house, the curtain falls.

Act III. The Great Hall in the Play-house.

(1) The masquerade is in full swing, everybody is in high spirits and there is much noisy hilarity. (2) The cotillon takes its beginning and after some minutes a couple leaves the

general round dance. (3) It is Leander with his beloved, who now tell each other their names—hers is Leonora—and promise each other that these names will always respond in joyful harmony. (4) In the meantime, Henrik has taken a fancy to Pernille, Leonora's maid, so they too have something to confide to each other. (5) A third couple leaves the crowd: it is Mr Leonard who is making passes at Mrs Magdelone, who is shamelessly telling him that she has neither husband nor child. Their tête-à-tête is on the point of ending in disaster when Mr Jeronimus interrupts it in his search for Leander. Thanks to the mask, however, he does not recognize his wife, but her dalliance with Mr Leonard has been interrupted. (6) A quarrel is brewing between students and officers but luckily the master of ceremonies announces the evening's entertainment, whose first item is the cock's dance. During this lively dance Henrik finds out who is wearing the Bacchus mask, (8) and he loses no time in telling his master about his discovery. The situation is critical, but Henrik finds a way out. (9) He asks the leader of the students, an elderly don, for help, telling him of Leander's plight. The don at once sides with the two young men; he asks Mr Jeronimus to drink a glass of wine with him with the purpose of making him drunk. (10) Arv, who has become the butt of the students' practical jokes, recognizes Henrik in the crowd and catches hold of him, but Henrik's threat of exposing him seals his lips. (11) Now follows the next item in the entertainment, which consists in the dancing master and his fiancée acting the story of Mars and Venus. Amid the general applause following this number, Jeronimus, who is by now not a little intoxicated, is drawn into a round dance by this couple, (12) while the students sing a song. During the round dance the old gentleman makes a complete fool of himself by (13) making passes at the dancing master's fiancée. Thus he attracts everybody's attention and (14) is told off by the students' chorus. The hour of general unmasking approaches. (15) The master of ceremonies, dressed as Corporal Mors[27], has a big urn placed in the middle of the floor and calls on everybody to throw their masks into it. (16) A feeling of mild sadness pervades the crowd while they file past the urn two by two. Not until now do the amazed Mr Leonard and Mrs Magdelone recognize each other, and when Leonora and Leander have also unmasked themselves it is almost a family reunion. The only one missing is Mr Jeronimus, who fuddled as he is, does not immediately understand that all has ended well: Leonora is Mr Leonard's daughter. But all further explanations are cut short by the master of ceremonies, who announces the break-up dance, during which Henrik (17) steps forward to address the audience and solicit their applause.

Already the two main themes of the overture[28] are typical of two sides of the opera: the racy side and the 'polite' side, but none of these themes returns later. The small arabesque, however, which opens the overture does return.

Ex. 6

It is the masquerade motif, which we find again in several places in acts I and III. First we meet it in the orchestra during Leander's awakening (3,2,2). It is immediately succeeded by another motif (3,3,4) which we shall get to know better later on.

Ex. 7

27] A hussar in black uniform with white braids. 28] P. t. o.

For the time being it provides a background for the short scene in which Henrik —half asleep—is recalling the joys of the previous evening. Here we have a genuine buffo: the play across the footlights; but no further than to the orchestra pit this time, and the musicians readily comply with his request to strike up the cotillon. This gives rise to a short dancing scene which is stopped by Leander's slapping Henrik's face. As a contrast to this piece of heftiness, a short lyrical arietta with a suggestion of the *lied* form (aba) is introduced. Also in what follows, exx. 6 and 7 play an important part. The latter very fittingly furnishes the music for Henrik's arietta "Alas, is it true?" (10,4,2). Now it is Leander's turn again (14,2,2), but we do not get more than a hint, for the situation (accompanied by ex. 6) begins to become somewhat delicate. Henrik tells his master just how delicate in a short charade, which ends in the court for matrimonial cases and whose patter recitation is quite like that met with in the buffa. An illustrative full stop is effectively furnished by the orchestra. Not surprisingly Leander's reaction is a lyrical arietta and no more surprisingly Henrik's description of the girls whose acquaintance he has made at the masquerade is characterized by a raciness which unfolds itself in an aba-form.

The dialogue in the first scene of the opera moves extremely rapidly; this means that as to form, the arioso passages are most frequently only hinted at (they are all tripartite). The only fully developed number in the scene is Henrik's charade. The tempo of the dialogue may have been influenced by 'Falstaff', but in the cleverly arranged contrasts Nielsen is absolutely original. The way in which he creates the atmosphere of a wealthy middle-class home in 1723 is quite original too.

This atmosphere becomes intensified in the second scene of the act, where Mrs Magdelone gives samples of her dancing skill. The orchestra opens the scene with a gavotte which, however, is elastic enough to allow itself to be varied in order to illustrate the dances Mrs Magdelone enumerates while she dances and sings. But the basis has to undergo a complete change when she goes on to dance a solemn *folie d'Espagne* (when, in other words, she passes from duple to triple time). Towards the end of the scene Henrik's enthusiasm overflows in a quotation of ex. 7, and there is hardly any doubt that the two young men would have given up their ironical attitude to Mrs Magdelone's performance had it not been abruptly ended by Mr Jeronimus' arrival. He well knows what is the matter with his wife and so does the orchestra: with mounting excitement (40,1,1) it quotes the motif from the beginning of the overture (ex. 6) while it furnishes Mrs Magdelone's lines with a background in the shape of the dance themes. Jeronimus' monologue, which follows immediately after, ends with a song with two stanzas ("In bygone days the street was peaceful").

Mr Leonard is introduced with a motif (54,1,3) which, as we shall meet it again, we may call the 'bow motif'.

28] There are two versions of the overture: the one which opens the opera and a concert version with a different ending.

Ex. 8

To the accompaniment of this motif the two old gentlemen reach an agreement
(60,1,1) and to this motif Arv greets Mr Leonard (I,6-62,2,3). Arv's stupidity is
illustrated by the lack of textual and musical variation in his lines. Now it is the
two young sinners' turn. Henrik begins by beating about the bush in a torrent of
words not unlike Rossini's patter arias. This torrent is formally an aa₁bb₁a₂ pattern
and it leads directly on to a ditty with two stanzas in varied strophic form
("In this country—" 69,2,4) which ends with enthusiastic praise of the masquerades, again with a quotation from ex. 7. When Henrik now has to justify his,
the servant's, going to the masquerade, he very logically begins (73,4,1) with
a repetition of the tune to "In this country—", for again the unsalubrious Danish
climate has to serve as an excuse. But he cannot use this tune when he goes on to
his "pro secundo", which describes the life of a poor boy—"We are born in poverty, we are swaddled in hunger"—with the hospitable ending: "You who are cold
out there, come in and be our guest". This part is composed as a dancing song in
fandango rhythm. In the first part of this song only the melody suggests its
character, but in the description of the masquerade procession the rhythm is
firmly established by the orchestra. This is no less than a stroke of genius, for it
ensures that the sudden departure from pure comedy caused by Henrik's social
criticism remains an integral part of the incident. Leander and Henrik now begin
their apology to Mr Leonard with arioso formalities, but are soon checked by
Mr Jeronimus' firm dictation. Their refusal to promise that Leander will marry
Mr Leonard's daughter leads on to the finale quintet (83,1,2), a breath-taking
altercation in which the two parties contradict each other in one and the same
rhythmically striking theme. Just as its possibilities seem to be exhausted, a new,
legato theme breaks through (90,2,6) and here it is worth noticing that the
otherwise somewhat yielding Leander is the one who introduces it while Henrik
only follows his lead. In spite of the fact that the old theme tries to hold its own,
Leander, closely followed by Henrik, succeeds in carrying through the new theme
to victory in the stretta: the young generation has demonstrated its independence.

This first act is quite a little masterpiece. It is very varied, but the variations
have a firm logical basis in the plot. It is rich in musical content, but this
never brings the action to an unnecessary standstill. But the best part of it is
that the comic effects and their musical illustrations are all the time derived
naturally from the situations, in which the characters never do anything not in
keeping with their masks.

After the presentation in act I of most of the characters and after this act
has introduced the intrigue, it is now up to act II to get the plot under weigh:
the young men must fool Jeronimus and Arv, his watchdog.

Act II opens with a prelude illustrative of night in Copenhagen in the 18th century, a lovely piece of music fraught with poetry, yet transparently clear in its formal construction (ABA₁). After the watchman has finished his song (the tune is Nielsen's own) the frightened Arv tries to fortify himself against his fear of the dark by singing a hymn, but is more comforted by thoughts of good food. These thoughts are the subject of a strophic song consisting of two stanzas with refrain (111,2,1). The tune bears a strong resemblance to the Danish 'singspiel' ditties. But his mood of well-being is brought to an abrupt end by the appearance of the ghost (II,2) and now the orchestra lets itself go in all sorts of illustrative pranks. During Arv's confessions the recitative imperceptibly takes on a ditty-like melodiousness and when we reach 'cook's virginity' (118,3,3), it attaches itself to a striking motif. The duet which follows takes its starting point in this motif and the orchestra furnishes the combining element. (II,3) Students, officers and girls are on their way to the play-house; they all tease Arv. The students sing their song in a simple *lied* form and that of the officers is a sterner variety of the same tune; they are both sung in unison. The girls, on the other hand, sing a three-part strophic song with two stanzas. Only Mr Leonard is kept away by Arv's presence for all Henrik has to do is to repeat 'cook's . . .', then the way is open to him and his master. They are not even in a hurry: Leander has time enough for a romanza (133,4,1) about the difference between his father's dark and gloomy house and the brightly illuminated play-house. And this is not all, for his meeting with Leonora (II,4) must naturally give rise to a duet.

It is quite obvious that this duet caused Nielsen certain difficulties for the scene has not one but two new characters viz. Leonora and Pernille, her maid, and of course Pernille too must make herself heard. As a matter of fact, we have here the makings of a quartet which might profitably have been constructed on a Mozartian pattern: the lyrical couple contrasted with the more prosaic couple. Instead we get a duet whose pattern is disturbed by the presence of Henrik and Pernille. There is nothing illogical here from the librettist's point of view: an introduction in which Leander, so to speak, welcomes Leonora, and Pernille, Henrik. Then a modest line from Leonora and a suggestion from Leander that she be less formal and say 'thou' to him[29]. They are united in a 'thou', kiss each other and rejoice in their love.

Nielsen has arranged this sequence of events in the following way: introduction from Leander (137,4,1), a lyrical andantino which is interrupted by a new motif in Pernille's brief line (138,3,3). After that Leonora opens the duet (139,3,1) to the following theme:

Ex. 9

29] There are two pronouns of address in Danish: 'du' and 'De' of which the former is less formal than the latter, cp. French 'tu' and 'vous'.

96

"Maskarade." I. act: Magdelone's dancing scene. From the left: Leander (Hans Kjerulf), Jeronimus (Karl Mantzius), Magdelone (Jonna Neiiendam), Henrik (Helge Nissen).

The Board of Directors of The Royal Academy of Music, 1917. From the left: Godfred Hartmann, Axel Gade, Anton Svendsen, A. P. Weis, Carl Nielsen.

Leander carries on this theme (140,3,1) and Leonora ventures her 'thou' first timidly, then more confidently. Together they rejoice in their sudden intimacy in sweet-sounding sixths:

Ex. 10

The kisses are exchanged on a new motif (143,2,4) and then the 'thou' motif returns in literal quotation (as in ex. 10). During all this Pernille and Henrik have been silent but by no means inactive spectators. The stage direction is: "During these hypersensitive fermatas Henrik and Pernille make parodic gestures in the background". But the theme with its sweet sixths and 'hypersensitive', often repeated fermatas is in itself a parody *all'italiana* of the original thought as—NB! —it was first formulated by *Leonora* (ex. 9). All this parody confuses us: are their declarations of love not seriously meant? If it is just an ordinary masquerade flirtation, why, then, Leander's refusal to marry another? Here it seems that Nielsen's sense of logic has let him down.

For the scene at the mask seller's (II,5) Nielsen has composed a strophic song with elements of typical hawkers' cries. He has not been able to resist the temptation to make the man a little tipsy. In the scene between Magdelone and Leonard (II,6) the dainty tripping is caught up in the orchestra's march-like tune, which returns when Leonard offers her his arm and they go to the masquerade together. It is a very angry Jeronimus who emerges from the mask shop together with Arv. In abruptly cut-off phrases he declares war on the crowd (158,2,1) and then in a strophic song with two stanzas he strikes a heroic attitude; the shape of this song reminds us of a patriotic song. It is parodied by Arv. The mask seller begins his song again, but breaks off and closes his shop. The watchman returns announcing the stroke of nine; behind his song we hear the dance music from the play-house, a quotation from the duet between Arv and Henrik (II,2).

There is no denying the fact that the tempo decreases considerably in this second act. The many incidents with people crossing the street are necessary to explain the presence of the various characters at the masquerade in act III, but there are many purely decorative elements: the watchman, the students, the officers, the girls and the mask seller; they all have a delaying effect and the cuts made in later performances (among other things of the mask seller's song and Jeronimus' 'heroic' song) are by no means unjustified.

In act III elements that have to do with the plot are few and far between. In many cases they are nothing but elaborations of the constellations which are already known to us from act II. This is true of scenes 3, 4 and 5. But also

97

scene 10, in which Henrik silences Arv, is a repetition. New constellations, however, are: Henrik/the don—the don/Jeronimus (scene 9)—Jeronimus/Venus (scene 13), and also the confrontation of the couples during the unmasking scene (scene 16).

Scenes 3, 4 and 5 are all duets (for practical reasons later productions of the opera have made use of a change of scene to a small room). Leonora's and Leander's duet (scene 3) is the one which is most elaborate formally. Leander begins (191,4,2) by asking Leonora to tell him her name (A). Leonora does so, and asks Leander to tell her his (B), after this they promise each other that these names will resound in eternal harmony (C). All three sections consist of two parts. Thus B consists of two stanzas in strophically varied form. In the first part of C there is a recall to the motif from the first part of A—this is psychologically right for it means that Leonora follows Leander, using his tune and after that (in the second part of C) both their voices are combined in a new tune. In the intensively lyrical tone of this duet there is none of the parody we saw in their first duet (II,4). The parody returns in scene 4, where Henrik and Pernille sing their *canzone parodica*. Its tune begins (198,1,2) as a travesty of Leander's tune from the preceding duet accompanied by a droll, rigid rhythm and harmony. This *canzone* is naturally much shorter than the duet. Pernille is not inhibited by maidenly bashfulness so she snatches the initiative immediately after Henrik's first phrase. They, too, exchange names, but this does not take place without a few puns which undulate back and forth between them in variations with Spanish colouring (possibly the fundamental rhythm also contains traces of Spanish influence). The third duet (scene 5) is altogether different from the other two, for here an older couple, Magdelone and Leonard, are engaged in amorous conversation behind their masks and Nielsen's mixture of amorousness and polite conversation is no less than masterly (203,2,4). In the accompaniment we hear themes from the beginning of the act (one of them derived from ex. 6); this is meant to indicate that this *risqué* scene would be unthinkable were it not for the abandoned atmosphere of the masquerade. We have no means of saying whether Magdelone's chastity would be able to withstand the attacks launched upon it, for her tête-à-tête with Leonard is interrupted by Jeronimus (207,2,2), who in one 'lied' phrase begs their pardon for his mistake.

The scene in which Henrik asks the don for help (scene 9) is a strophic song with no less than five stanzas. However, the strophic form is varied so that all the stanzas begin in the same way (and with an orchestra quotation of ex. 6), but continue in different ways. This results in a kind of rondo. In two of the sections there is a motif (226,2,1) which we hear again later in the don's invitation to Jeronimus (231,1,2); this logically associates the suggestion of the idea with its execution. This motif is also quoted in the following scene (scene 10) resulting in an even firmer association with Bacchus/Jeronimus. This scene between Arv and Henrik is otherwise dominated by the theme from "cook's..." (118,3,3), which the orchestra hammers out during four measures so that even

98

the stupid Arv is left in no doubt. The plan to neutralize Jeronimus (propounded in scenes 9 and 10) proves to have been very effective in scene 13. The rather tipsy Jeronimus makes up to Venus in a song-like strain full of illustrative features which all allude to his intoxication (262,1,1).

The unmasking scene is of an unusual sensitivity in this otherwise racy act. Throughout 33 measures the orchestra plays music of a three-level structure. At the bottom we have the double organ point (E flat—B flat) of the deep parts; the inner parts add an ostinato motif of one bar and in the treble we hear another ostinato motif. As the main characters walk past the urn, the motif of the violins yields to motifs which have at some point been associated with each of them. Only Jeronimus is given no memory motif in spite of the fact that he at once becomes his old truculent self when he discovers Henrik, Leander and his wife. But when he also finds Mr Leonard in their midst he becomes a little embarrassed and now the 'bow motif' is introduced again (ex. 8). The *dénouement* is disposed of without much ado. It is as if Jeronimus' amazement transmits itself to composer as well as librettist, and both hurry towards the final curtain.

It would be unfair to call this act static, it is crowded with incident, only most of it has nothing whatever to do with the plot. Of the seventeen scenes in the act nine are purely decorative[30]. This is true of scene 1: the general chorus of those taking part in the masquerade, scene 2: the cotillon (a round dance of the polka type), scene 6: the quarrel between students and officers, scene 7: the cock's dance (this is one of the greatest triumphs of Nielsen's fertile imagination: within the frame work of the polonaise he gives a great number of comically illustrative traits, all inspired by the poultry yard. In its coda, ex. 7 becomes fully developed). The second divertissement, the pantomime (scene 11) is also decorative and scene 12, the don's dancing song (with nine (!) stanzas) does not contribute to the development of the plot either. This scene ends with the students' ovation of Jeronimus in the drinking song: "Og dette skal være . . ." (And this is in honour of . . .). The tune to this song has its origin in a popular German 18th century tune (this is the only quotation in the opera and as we see, there is no anachronism). But as the students, too, are in their cups they have difficulty in agreeing about the key. Scenes 14 and 15 are also decorative. The first of these is a strophic chorus song with three stanzas. It ends with the refrain from the don's dancing song (scene 12) and thus becomes attached to the following scene, in which Corporal Mors travesties the same ditty after an introduction in the shape of a funeral march. Scene 17 is the finale of the opera and also of the masquerade: it is a dance chorus in which only one of the main characters viz. Henrik has a solo. He steps forward to the footlights and addresses the audience. He starts with a theme from the break-up dance but leaves it in order (281,1,4) to quote his song "In this country" (I,6-69,2,4), in which he solicits the applause of the onlookers and expresses the hope that in spite of frost, snow,

30] This abundance of scenes with decorative function has been partly remedied by means of cuts in later performances.

7*

storm and fog, the play has been able to warm their souls and make them think of summer.

In 'Maskarade' there are many features common to all opera comedy: Henrik's appeal to the orchestra (5,2,4), patter parlando (66,2,3), chromatic misery (57,1,2) and numerous illustrative touches, especially in the orchestra. In fact, there is hardly a single original idea in the whole of 'Maskarade'. Yet, there can be no doubt that the work has a character all its own. This is principally due to Nielsen's musical personality, of which every single part of the opera bears the stamp; but it is also due to the fact that Nielsen, when reaching back for inspiration to a time before the immediately preceding generation, drew on the Danish 'vaudeville', which stood in full bloom about 1830 and in which, in his capacity of opera violinist, he had taken part. In the analysis of 'Maskarade' we have seen that the strophic form (either varied or merely suggested) is among his favourites. To this must be added two typical features of his strophic songs: the ditty-like character of their melody and their dance-like elements which characterize its rhythm even when it is not attached to a definite dance rhythm. As the Danish 'vaudeville' is an offshoot of the French vaudeville comedy, it is not surprising that 'Maskarade' is also indebted to the opéra comique. The absence of vocal brilliance is French and so is the pains taken with the declamation. The decorative choruses are French in their origin and also the chorus finale of act III with its direct appeal to the audience. However, Nielsen did not want to imitate the spoken dialogue typical of the opéra comique; and in his melodious recitative with its close affinity to the intonation of the Danish language, we have one of the more easily definable elements of the opera's distinctively Danish character.

In spite of its success[31] 'Maskarade' was Nielsen's last opera. An offer of collaboration in a new opera from Professor Frants Buhl was turned down: "I don't think I shall get round to opera for some time."[32] And when Vilhelm Andersen gave him another libretto in 1922, he could not get into his stride, one reason being that it seemed to him that the subject matter—Holberg's 'Kilderejsen' (the excursion to the spring)—was so close to 'Maskarade' that there would be danger of repetition. Once more—on the occasion of Hans Andersen's 125th anniversary in 1930—he toyed with the idea of writing an opera. The subject was to have been the fairy tale 'Den uartige Dreng' (the naughty boy) as dramatized by Sophus Michaëlis, who had made use of Andersen's love for Jenny Lind, the famous singer. No opera came of this, but a small play 'Amor og Digteren' (Cupid and the poet), for which Carl Nielsen composed an overture, some incidental music and a few songs.

Many are the plays that in the course of time he enriched with music of

---

31] 20 performances in the first season, 1906—7; 50th performance on 25.11.1925; 100th performance on 18.3.1946.

32] Letters p. 97.

various kinds. Many of his immensely popular songs were heard for the first time from the stage and not a few of his popular orchestra pieces were written to illuminate dramatic incidents. But in most cases Nielsen devoted his energies to writing wonderful music to plays which have now sunk into oblivion.

It is remarkable that even in cases where he attached his name to that of the greatest figure of our golden age: Oehlenschläger[33], music and drama did not become an organic whole to the same extent as Kuhlau's music and 'Elver-høj' (The Elf-Hill) or Lange-Müller's music and 'Der var engang—' (once upon a time—); these two plays would be unthinkable without their music. Could it be because Nielsen's music is not contemporary with the works to which he wrote it? The fault is definitely not in the quality of the music—the reason must be that it does not present itself as the only possibility as is the case with Kuhlau's and Lange-Müller's music.

We must seek consolation in the fact that the music dramatist takes leave of the opera at the very moment when the symphonist grows into full stature. Possibly this is a contributory cause.

33] We are thinking of his music to 'Hagbart og Signe' (1910), 'Sankt Hansaftenspil' (1913) and 'Aladdin' (1918).

(Translated by Hans Hartvigson
and Norman M. Shine)

THE CHORAL WORKS

by

Søren Sørensen

The tradition of great choral compositions in Danish music dates from the end of the eighteenth century when Danish music began to display distinctive features of its own. Musical life on a higher level centred round the Church and the Crown. A tradition, which continued during the nineteenth century, was founded with the cantatas which distinguished immigrant musicians wrote to celebrate special occasions during the ecclesiastical year or events in the Royal Family (chief among these Joh. Ad. Scheibe's cantata for the funeral of Frederik V, F. L. Æ. Kunzen's oratorio "Skabningens Halleluja" ("The Alleluja of Creation"), J. A. P. Schulz's "Kristi Død" ("The Death of Christ") and some ceremonial music). In 1819 C. E. F. Weyse was appointed Court composer, in which capacity it was his task to write cantatas for ecclesiastical and national festivals. This genre continued after Weyse's time but gradually developed a less official and more universal character.

In 1853 Niels W. Gade composed his lyrical choral ballad "Elverskud" ("Elf-shot"), the story of which is derived from a medieval ballad while the music deliberately approaches folk music. J. P. E. Hartmann and Peter Heise together with Gade are the most distinguished representatives of the romantic tradition, and from a stylistic point of view in clear and unambiguous sympathy with the German romantic movement (Schumann, Mendelssohn, L. Spohr and the early Wagner). In the 1860's and 70's choral music reaches its highwater mark in the works of these composers, and it has developed into a rather conventional and derivative kind of music when Carl Nielsen begins his career as a composer.

Nielsen wrote choral works fairly regularly throughout his life. Some of them are occasional cantatas (these continue on a common level the old tradition of the court and church cantata), others might be called free choral compositions written without any external cause and unconnected with any specific event or occasion. The latter group continues the freer lyrical tradition of choral composition, which had developed during the nineteenth century. On the following pages we shall concentrate on these 'freer' choral works.

The following is a complete list of the choral compositions of Carl Nielsen:

Hymnus amoris (words by Axel Olrik/J. L. Heiberg) 1896.
Cantata for the Lorenz Frølich Festival (Axel Olrik) 1900.
Cantata for the Students' Community (Holger Drachmann) 1902.
Sleep (Johannes Jørgensen) 1904.

Cantata for the anniversary of Copenhagen University (Niels Møller) 1908.
Cantata in commemoration of the year 1659 (L. C. Nielsen) 1909.
Cantata for the National Exhibition at Aarhus (L. C. Nielsen) 1909.
Cantata for the ceremony in memory of P. S. Krøyer (L. C. Nielsen) 1909.
Cantata for the centenary of the Merchants' Guild (Vald. Rørdam) 1917.
Springtime in Funen (Aage Berntsen) 1921.
Three Motets, 1929.
Cantata for the centenary of the Technical High School (H. H. Seedorff Pedersen) 1929.
Cantata for the fiftieth anniversary of the Young Merchants' Education Association (H. H. Seedorff Pedersen) 1930.
Cantata for the fiftieth anniversary of the Danish Cremation Society (Sophus Michaëlis) 1931.

The idea of the first of these works, "Hymnus amoris", originated in a visual experience (as did that of the 2nd symphony at a later date). On his honeymoon in 1891 Nielsen saw in Padua a picture by Tizian, the subject of which—a young man killing his love out of jealousy—made so strong an impression both on himself and on his wife that they formed the project of creating within their respective branches of art a work portraying love in all its aspects. The relief which Anne Marie Carl Nielsen planned was never executed, but the thought of this work and its musical working-out was brought to maturity in the mind of Carl Nielsen in the following years.

The work is characteristic of an important aspect of Nielsen's aesthestic view of music: his polemic attitude towards pure programme music, and the conception, to which he frequently gave expression, of music as an objective and universal language. This attitude is the reason why *Latin* was chosen for this work. In his preface to the work Nielsen says in explanation "that this language is of a monumental quality and elevates one above too lyrical and personal feelings which would not be fitting when portraying such a universally human force as love through the medium of a large polyphonic choral work". He emphasized the desire to be 'objective' and 'universal' in contrast to all that is too 'lyrical' and 'personal', a contrast typifying his position in relation to the prevailing tradition in Danish music at that time. His view of programme music and of programmes of art as a whole is also clearly expressed in the preface which begins with these words: "Although I think it best to let works of art, sculpture as well as painting and music, speak for themselves and in their own language, it is, nevertheless, necessary to say a few words especially with reference to the Latin text . . .".

Although in Latin the text is not an old one: it was written for the work, first in Danish by Axel Olrik, the folklorist, and then translated into Latin by Johan Ludvig Heiberg, the most distinguished classical scholar in Denmark at that time (not to be confused with the poet, his relative and namesake who was three generations older). Nielsen gives himself an account of the origin of the text: "The idea of having the different ages of man praise the power of love and of having it find its consummation and transfiguration in a reflection of the celestial is my own, but my warm thanks are due to Dr. Axel Olrik who has given the vague outlines of my idea form and colour in such a remarkable and powerful way, and to Professor J. L. Heiberg, who has given the result a definite form in his Latin translation."

The text consists entirely of fourlined stanzas. In the first four parts of the work—childhood, youth, manhood and old age—the first and the last lines of each stanza are identical, the other lines are unrhymed; all four lines of the last four stanzas, the 'celestial' part, are independent, and still unrhymed.

The work is written as one continuous whole, without any break between the parts, and the basis of the work is one single theme which is introduced right at the beginning (here given from the first vocal entry):

Ex. 1

In an account of the work which Nielsen gave in connection with a German performance (see Meyer and Schandorf Petersen, *Carl Nielsen*, p. 132) he motivates the idea behind the use of this theme which runs through the whole composition, and the structure of the work as a continuous whole: "Just as love is a feeling common to all men at all ages, so one musical theme is the basis for the whole structure of this work, and as the different ages of man pass imperceptibly from one to the other, so this hymn has no definite sections nor intermissions. The whole work progresses as one continuous sweep."

The unique position of the work among Danish choral compositions at the time of its appearance is evident from its polyphonic design. In the preceding years Nielsen had made intensive studies of polyphonic writing in the works of Palestrina, Bach, and Handel—and it is symptomatic that the work is dedicated to Orla Rosenhoff, his teacher of the theory of music at the Academy, and one of the very few teachers to have had any real influence on his development.

The polyphonic writing beautifully suits the musical language which is peculiar to Nielsen and which had been developed in the previous works, the 1st symphony, the string quartet in F minor, the sonata for violin in A major etc. It is characterized by a pure handling of melody with capricious features (see ex. 2) acting as a contrast to the real thematic material, couched in harmonies of which the triad is the basic element, ideologically founded on the conviction of the power of the simple intervals and the triad to give the music a universal and 'super'-personal expression.

Ex. 2

105

The first stanza, "Childhood", is written as a simple three-part setting for children's voices (see ex. 1) carried through note against note. It is the only section which is not polyphonic, corresponding to the simple, uncomplicated world of the child. The second stanza, the mothers' stanza, which speaks of the joy of bringing forth life and seeing it grow, has as its central part a fugue for four female voices on the theme (from ex. 1) with a small jubilant variation in the second bar. The fugue as a whole is a typical instance from Nielsen's early works of his gift for expressing himself with melodious warmth and rich tonal nuances within a thoroughly consistent diatonic writing.

Ex. 3

The children's stanza, a repetition of the first stanza in a slightly varied form, rounds off this section, "Childhood", thus producing a small ABA form. Then "Youth", the age of aspiring love, is given its stanza, built up in a rhythmic and dynamic crescendo, with the 'Sturm und Drang'-quality especially brought out in the accompaniment by pizzicato syncopations in the strings and by strong contrasts of tonality. This stanza also ends with a veritable fugue on the main theme in a slightly varied form, and in contrast to the four female voices of the previous stanza this one is written for four young men, four tenor voices.

When a maximum of tension has been reached in the freer, final part of the fugue, in which the brass stresses the culmination both as regards texture and dynamics, a relaxation sets in and the fugue gives way to the stanza of manhood, the proclamation of the clarified, calmly flowing, and ever invigorating love, expressed in a four-part fugue (for full men's chorus) with a simple, doubling accompaniment by the lower strings and wind instruments. The texture becomes increasingly full and florid till it is abruptly cut off by a strong contrast, the stanza of the unhappy woman. In his account of this passage Nielsen writes: "The men sing about exploits and strength, and the composer has chosen the virile fugal style in order to express the joy of work and feeling of strength. The continuation is an austere four-part fugal setting which is suddenly interrupted by the agonizing scream of a woman:

Amor est dolor meus,	Love is my affliction,
nil me altius vulneravit,	nothing has hurt me more,
nil tamen carius.	yet it is dear to me.
Amor est dolor meus.	Love is my affliction.

This throws, as it were, a shadow over the jubilant praise of love which till now has been the fundamental tone and forms a contrast with what went before and likewise with what follows. For she is not allowed to sing of affliction and sorrow for a very long time. Gradually a women's chorus sets in, and having tried to interrupt her time and again it gets the upper hand at last, and her lonely voice is drowned in the surge of music. Now the fugue of the men is resumed but this time joined by female voices."

The entry of the unhappy woman and the contrast as regards contents to what precedes, is stressed by the abrupt and jerky modulation from the main key of A major to the remote A flat major and by the violent dissonances at her entry:

Ex. 4

In accordance with Nielsen's intentions, as stated in his explanatory notes, this section forms a contrast to the surrounding stanzas. The lines of the unhappy woman interrupt the praise to the lifegiving power of love through all ages of human life and reveals in a flash the kindling and consuming fire — "yet it is dear to me". It is this element which gives a wider perspective to the hymn to love, the calmly burning flame has kindled a great conflagration in the heart of man, which he neither can nor will fly. This passage is akin to the text: "Charity believeth all things, hopeth all things, endureth all things".

By the resumption of the fugal stanza, the manhood stanza (now for five-part mixed chorus), a small complete ABA form is once more created within a section, marking at the same time a synthesis of the overwhelming and the organically flowing love (cf. Nielsen's explanatory notes), and in logical consequence the stanza of old age follows immediately: "Amor est pax mea", a fugue for three male voices.

The passage through the ages of man is now at an end and the idea of the final section of the work, which from a musical point of view is a sort of coda, is the union of the celestial choir of angels and the chorus of all mankind in a final praise of love. The children's voices of the first section of the work, now symbolizing the angelic choir, join the chorus of mankind in an eight-part double chorus on the love theme, the main theme of the work. The paean has been brought to an end, the classic fundamental principle of aesthetics, unity in multiplicity, has found an excellent expression in this work, in which unity is represented by the persistent and easily recognizable love theme, and multiplicity is created by the colourful variation of tonality, the polyphonic part-writing, and the dynamic effect.

Closely related to "Hymnus amoris" both in form and psychological idea is the choral composition "Sleep". It dates from the time between the composition of the two operas, the period of the 2nd symphony and the Helios overture. The thought of the nature of sleep, its quiet refreshing power, and its opposite, the lacerating nightmare, inspired Nielsen to this work (just as previously the praise of the power of love gained in profundity by the tension between the calm lifegiving flame and the consuming fire). As in the case of "Hymnus amoris" Nielsen passes his idea on to a poet, who then writes his 'libretto' especially for the purpose. This time Nielsen turns to Johannes Jørgensen (1866—1956),—the previous year he had written one of his finest songs for Jørgensen's poem "Sænk kun dit hoved, du blomst" (Lower your head, o flower).

The work, written as one continuous whole, consists of three parts without any break. The composer has been especially absorbed by the central part, the nightmare, and both quantitatively and qualitatively this part has been most fully worked out. Nielsen, the dramatist (the work is temporally close to the two operas) avails himself in this section of an abundance of strong musical effects in order to reproduce the horrors of a nightmare, while the surrounding sections, depicting sleep as the calmly burning flame, the symbol of life's growth, which was the main thing in "Hymnus amoris", here serve as a background to the colourful music of the nightmare. The work is thus built up as a great, ever increasing tension culminating at the end of the nightmare section, at which point the agony of fear puts on its stranglehold; then the music is relaxed and returns like the text to a continuation of the quiet sleep of the beginning.

The beginning and the end of the poem are written in a gently rocking trochaic rhymed metre, while it is less regular in the great central part: long and short lines alternate and the rhythm changes in order to depict the hag-ridden tossing about. The musical treatment is in principle polyphonic, but here a freer polyphony is used without any sustained fugue-episodes, and with effective passages of a more declamatory, homophonic texture.

The beginning is characterized as regards both melody and tonality by a groping, slightly restless quality, and has a triplet in the main theme which plays an important part throughout the opening section:

Ex. 5

This section fades out on the passage "Happy the man who sleeps", and when the music has been brought to rest on a peaceful C major chord, a violin-tremolo sets in; with the entry of the following voices the key is dislocated from its secure position in C minor-C major to a centreless tonal flinging around, and sharp and piercing dissonances set in with ever growing force at the same time as the character of the music by the sustained tremolo of the accompaniment is changed into a "Molto agitato", heralding the second section, Inferno: "An agony, a heaviness, woe is me, am I awake?".

Ex. 6

The whole of this section is one of the most subjectively coloured passages in Nielsen's work. Nowhere else has he so concentratedly and so relentlessly made

109

use of dissonances to serve expression. One intensely dissonant chord is succeeded by another in a continual musical ride, which, performed by the whole orchestra, crushes any consonance of the singing voices. A few bars from the orchestral interlude before the final agony of fear sets in can serve as an illustration of the character of this ride:

Ex. 7

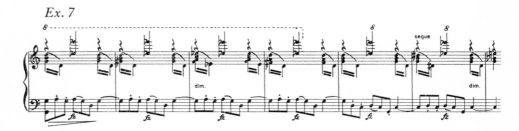

The chorus is treated sometimes in imitative, frequently in duo-imitative, phrases, sometimes in homophonic blocks of chords of a more declamatory nature, reaching their climax in the final bars:

Ex. 8

Gradually the tension is relaxed, the concentration and volume of the tremolo decrease and give way to gentler sounds and gentler instrumentation with solo-

110

istic playing by the melodic instruments, the flute and the violin, whose characteristic clearness of tone has been employed in a healing and soothing way in the
vegetating transitional bars, to the words: "Dreams vanish, visions fade, illu-
sions pass away". Then the triplet motive of the opening (ex. 5) returns in
a varied, more serene treatment symbolizing calm dreamless sleep: "Pious sleep,
our gentle mother / give me peace and rest again / let me in thy bosom find /
new strength, new smiles". The words of the beginning are repeated at the end
in the chaste, diatonically elaborated musical language, which is typical of Nielsen and which we in this connection recognize from "Hymnus amoris".

Ex. 9

"Søvnen" (Sleep) is exceptional among the choral compositions of Nielsen by
virtue of its strongly dramatic expressiveness. Before commencing this work he
had taken a special interest in the works of Max Reger, and it is possible that
the latter's strongly subjective musical language and peculiar ideas of form may
have influenced the central section, the nightmare-scene, but in the last analysis
it is Nielsen's classically orientated, aesthetic view of music which is the true
incentive. Here the stress is on the *tension* between what he calls the objective
musical language, rooted in the classic polyphonically orientated composers, and
its contrast, the relentless use of free dissonance to serve expressiveness, with its
resultant restlessness and frustration.

"Fynsk forår" (Springtime in Funen), the third of the 'free' choral compositions, does not aspire to be a profound psychological elucidation of one of the lifegiving forces in human life. The work is called a 'lyrical humoresque' and is a
cantata in miniature praising Funen, the composer's native island. This time the
poet was Aage Berntsen (1885—1952), also known as a doctor and born in Funen
himself. He was the son of Klaus Berntsen, the politician, who in 1883 introduced
Nielsen to the most distinguished people in the musical circles of the capital.

Nielsen did not himself sponsor the idea of this work. The text was submitted
for a competition arranged by the Danish Choral Society for a text describing
Danish nature, history, or life and manners, and Nielsen had promised to set music

111

to the prize text. "Fynsk forår" by Aage Berntsen was awarded the prize, and after having had the text in his possession for several years Nielsen set it to music in July—August 1921.

Although shorter than his earlier choral compositions this work is more cantata-like. There is no unifying theme running through the entire work; it consists of a series of independent sections although these are tied together by small orchestral transitions. Nielsen was quite conscious of the more conventional nature of the form scheme. In a letter dating from August 1921 he writes: "I am working on a choral composition with solos, orchestra and everything, which I promised 4 og 5 years ago to do for 'the united choral societies in Denmark'." The addition 'and everything' reveals his conception of it as a rather traditional cantata. And yet, in spite of conventions and in spite of the low spirits evident in the following part of the letter, it became one of the most sparkling and most spontaneously captivating works Nielsen ever wrote. It was written at the time when Nielsen's productivity of songs was at its height. In the years after 1914, when Nielsen began work on Danish songs in collaboration with Thomas Laub, and especially in 1920—21 (as seen from his letters from these years) he was continuously occupied in writing Danish songs, constantly encouraged to do so by people from the Danish Folk High School. The music for "Moderen" ("The Mother") also dates from 1920, and in this work we find some of his most representative songs.

The musical structure of "Fynsk forår" would hardly have been possible if he had not previously been intensely occupied with ballad-like songs. The work is a collection of songs magnified for public performance, alternating between choral and solo interpretation, and with an orchestral accompaniment first and foremost lending choral support and, moreover, in the more vivacious sections having a characterizing function in depicting the undulating fields and the scenery of Funen. The choruses are in principle homophonic with a leading upper voice and a 'lied'-like division into periods, and the solo passages are likewise 'lied'-like, frequent use being made of the alternation between major and minor thirds, which is characteristic of the diatonic writing of Nielsen.

Ex. 10

A tendency to dramatic treatment can be seen in the confrontation of the girl and the young man, in her song about the wistful heart, and in his lyrical ballad expressing his adoration of Ilsebil, the neighbour's daughter; but the love dreams of spring are only suggested and the idyll remains unbroken. The blind musician, whom the old Klaus Berntsen knew as a child, is also part of this picture of spring in Funen. So is the refrain of the girls, in Denmark especially attributed to the girls of Funen: "The night is our own". These words are used as the pianissimo-pianissimo-refrain of the only contrapuntal section of the work, in which an exquisite twilight atmosphere is painted by the terzet: "See, apple-blossoms are falling in the lane / the night is our own", sung by the soloists (soprano, tenor, and baritone).

The musical form is, as in all his songs, closely allied to the lyrical conception of nature and the popular song tradition which go back to J. A. P. Schulz, singled out for special mention by both Nielsen and Laub as the true pattern for the style of popular songs. "Fynsk forår" is evidently in the direct line of descent from "Peter's Wedding" and "The Harvest Festival", the Danish 'singspiele' by Schulz cf. the opening of the final dancing song in "Fynsk forår" (ex. 11). Six years later his musical praise of Funen, the island where Carl Nielsen had spent his childhood, gets its literary counterpart on a larger scale in his memoirs "Min fynske barndom" (My Childhood in Funen).

Ex. 11

Only a few of the ten cantatas which he had been commissioned to write for special occasions have been published. The best of these—prominence must be given to the University Cantata written to the powerful words by Niels Møller—contain passages of great musical beauty and imposing choral sections, but a more detailed account of these works is not possible here. Finally we shall consider a group of works which stands apart from the other choral compositions of Nielsen, viz. the three a cappella motets which he wrote during the last years of his life.

113

Here, too, it is the conception of the qualities of classical choral polyphony, its 'super'-personal, musical expressiveness of universal validity, which has fascinated him. This time the occasion was some concerts given by the Palestrina Choir conducted by Mogens Wöldike with a programme consisting of classical motets from the fifteenth and sixteenth centuries. Founded in 1924, the Palestrina Choir won a widespread fame in 1928 by winning the prize in an international choral competition in Milano, and for many years Nielsen followed the activities of the chorus at close quarters. He was prompted by the concerts of the chorus to become once more deeply absorbed in the art of vocal polyphony, and at the request of Mogens Wöldike he wrote the three motets for the Palestrina Choir to which they were dedicated.

Only the framework of classical choral art has been employed, there is no instrumental accompaniment, and the form is that of the true motet in which each textual section serves for a point of imitation and the polyphonic treatment of the sections alternates between a freer and a more strict kind. In the classic tradition is, moreover, the choice of words, passages from three Psalms, which particularly attracted Nielsen; and the Latin language, the objevtive church language, was likewise retained.

"Afflictus sum, et humiliatus sum nimis: rugiebam a gemitu cordis mei" ("I am feeble and sore smitten: I have roared for the very disquietness of my heart"), the first of the motets, is written for four deep voices, contralto, tenor I-II, bass, to render vocally the profound horror and fear of death which are expressed in the words. The effect produced by the tense dissonances is related to that of the nightmare-section of "Søvnen", but it has been used with considerably more restraint in the motet. This consists of two sections, each divided into halves, the last section being a shortened repetition of the first (ABab). The B-section with the exclamation "Rugiebam" in short phrases and the violent dissonances, has an impressive, mysteriously fascinating effect. The dissonance built on whole-tone intervals is a sound effect which is new in Nielsen, but which became widely used by the following generation of composers as a means of expression.

Ex. 12

The other two motets are written for the normal set of voices, soprano, contralto, tenor, and bass. They are lighter in tone corresponding to the contents of the text. No. 2 is of a pastoral character ("Dominus regit me...", "The Lord is my shepherd..."). The third is throughout like a hymn of praise ("Benedictus...", "Blessed be the Lord..."). As a contrast to the short, meek, almost groping phrases of the first, agonized motet (ex. 12) serves in the last one the exultant praise with its long unburdened breath, expressed in lengthy phrases with melismatic elaborations and in a polyphonic texture reflecting Nielsen's conception of objectivity and universal validity.

Ex. 13

Considered in relation to other genres, the choral compositions of Nielsen can hardly be said to be of primary importance among his works, but even if he had written nothing else, they would have secured him a permanent position in the history of Danish music. With these works he has, in a way entirely his own, reanimated a form of art which was often treated in a most traditional way. Especially in these works his independence of his immediate predecessors and older contemporaries is evident. He has entered thoroughly into the spirit of classic polyphonic music, avoiding the prevailing tradition and metamorphosing the models chosen into a form of expression which, as pointed out above, in every detail reflects his conception of music as art and his emphasis on restraint and 'objectivity' in order that tension and passions can be the more powerful when called forth.

(Translated by Ruth Bentzen)

THE SONGS

by

NILS SCHIØRRING

Have you noticed how many modern composers have, as it were, approached music from the wrong side? They begin with the scent, the poetry, the flower, the height of their art instead of starting with the roots, the soil, the planting, and the propagation. In other words: they begin by expressing moods, feelings, colours, and sensations instead of studying part-writing and counterpoint and so forth. But in this respect, I admit I am rather old-fashioned and I do not think that I can change my ideas. —

It was shortly after New Year 1911, at the same time as his "Sinfonia Espansiva" was nearing completion, that Carl Nielsen, even then recognized as the great and strange though not unconditionally admired modernist in Danish music, wrote thus to his slightly younger Swedish friend and fellow artist, the pianist and composer, Wilhelm Stenhammar. His remarks were occasioned by a discussion between the two older composers about the young Swedish composer, Ture Rangström. Nielsen admitted that Rangström had the gift of giving his music scent and poetic colour, but he was afraid that the young Swede's talent was not founded "on a truly elementary basis, musculature, or whatever one can call it".

Both in form and content this kind of remark is typical of Nielsen. It amused him, when later in life young students of music showed him a detailed analysis of his works. Even the most complicated and artistically consistent development in his symphonic works was not primarily the result of a conscious, preconceived plan, but had developed organically from the first entry of the first theme with a strict musical sense of form.

Above all, he was guided by his sense of inner balance. His art was the result of deep reflection, not in an analytical but in a constructive sense, which was based not only on a natural sensibility to melodic and harmonic elements, but which also grew out of an observant and—for a composer of his time, Danish or foreign—quite unusual familiarity with the tone language of earlier ages, Gregorian chant, the vocal polyphony of the fifteenth and sixteenth centuries, and genuine, not arranged folk music. This background made his ear sensitive not only to the renewal or rejuvenation which the late-Romantic music of his day might fetch from other melodic ideals, but he also gained an intimate knowledge of systems other than the major-minor tonal system, which, although it was on

117

the verge of reaching its ultimate point, nevertheless still formed the basis of practically all musical composition.

At a very early stage he himself encouraged young composers who sought his advice to study counterpoint and to seek out the old masters, and in his own first works the outcome of his immersion in basic compositional elements is evident. Many years later, this immersion resulted in the often quoted passage from his collection of essays, "Levende Musik" (Living Music): "a melodic third should be regarded as a divine gift, a fourth as an experience, and a fifth as the greatest joy. Thoughtless greed undermines health".

These were the words of a composer who, practically until his death, was regarded by his contemporaries as an ultra-Radical and an experimentalist; he not only formulated these tenets, he lived by them. He was an innovator in Danish music, joining together past and present behind what had become the late-Romantic tradition.

It was above all in his songs that Nielsen was able to follow his theory that the fundamental thing was the simplicity of the tune and a faithful interpretation of the text. But to begin with he met with little understanding. He wrote his earliest songs in an atmosphere pervaded by quite other traditions than those which he upheld. The fusion in his early songs of a melodically clear structure with an advanced harmonic accompaniment shocked his contemporaries, and his songs were called distortions and were said to be the expression of a morbid desire for independence. The song tradition which was being so zealously guarded had reached its culmination with Heise's romances, was continued by Lange-Müller, and willingly carried on by lesser composers.

It was indeed not so very long ago that the simple ballad-like airs, of which Carl Nielsen and Thomas Laub were to become the most eminent exponents in the twentieth century, had ruled almost absolutely. The influence from the German romantic songs with piano accompaniment, the 'lieder' of Schubert and Schumann, which we generally call romances, was late. The simple, popular airs of the late eighteenth century with their touch of the familiar, which we owe to J. A. P. Schulz (who lived and worked in Copenhagen from 1787 to 1795), had been handed down to his pupil, C. E. F. Weyse. Weyse composed more subjectively sensitive and romantically coloured tunes to his more lyrical romantic songs. Many of Weyse's songs were originally composed for *singspiele* or operas, and it is in this field that the romance develops towards the Romantic tradition, with a more colourful and sonorous accompaniment, but without ever penetrating or illuminating the text, as Schubert did with such genius in his very first Goethe songs. The progressive songs of Kuhlau, who in a far higher degree than Weyse turned his ear outwards to the world around him and who, also presumably because he was younger, was far more susceptible to new influences, left little impression, it was so clearly Schulz' and Weyse's influence which dominated the Danish song while, at the same time, certain elements of a rather flowery lyrical nature were being imported from foreign operas and *singspiele*. These elements

118

may be found in some of Rudolph Bay's songs, e.g. "Du er rig, du er dejlig, o Syd" (Thou art rich, thou art lovely, O South), in J. P. E. Hartmann's "Flyv Fugl, flyv" (Fly, bird, fly), Henrik Rung's "I Danmark er jeg født" (In Denmark I was born), and the young Niels W. Gade's "Lette Bølge, naar du blaaner" (Light wave, when thou colourest).

The strophic song was by far the most predominant type; far rarer was the through composed song, which was mostly used to ballad texts, e.g. Gade's "Knud Lavard" (1842) and "Hvorfor svulmer Weichselfloden" (Wherefore swells the Weichsel River) (1849), which again are inspired more by Schumann's "Die beiden Grenadiere" than by the professional German ballad composers of the Romantic Age, Löwe in particular. The musical aim in these strophic songs was primarily the pretty tune. The relationship between the text and the tune was only faintly perceived; the tune was presumably composed with a certain vague sentimental regard for the text, but the connection between text and tune was still practically as in the Pre-Romantic songs, where there was an appreciable distance between the two.

Schubert's and Schumann's romantic *lieder* were not known in Denmark at all until Gade, after his appointment as conductor and artistic director of the Musikforeningen (the Musical Society) quite naturally included in his programmes the songs which he had come to know and love during his years in Leipzig. And when Heise, who was to become the greatest name in the art of the Danish romance for the next twenty-five years, published his first songs at the beginning of the 1850s, these were also strophic songs with a closer resemblance to popular songs than to romances. It was not until he returned from his stay in Leipzig that Heise gradually developed into a fully-fledged Romantic composer of romances with a wonderful gift for describing both the hushed mood and the colourfully dramatic in a romantic fusion of the song and the piano accompaniment.

When one considers Nielsen's immense importance to the Danish song in the twentieth century, the collections of songs which he published independently do not amount to much. They are "Musik til fem Digte af J. P. Jacobsen", op. 4, 1892 (Music to Five Poems by J. P. Jacobsen), "Viser og Vers af J. P. Jacobsen", op. 6, 1893 (Songs and Verse by J. P. Jacobsen), "Seks Sange" (Ludvig Holstein), op. 10, 1897 (Six Songs), "Strofiske Sange", I—II, op. 21, 1907 (Strophic Songs), "En Snes danske Viser" I—II (A Score of Danish Songs—in collaboration with Th. Laub) no op., 1915 and 1917, "Tyve folkelige Melodier" (Twenty Popular Melodies) no op., 1921, "Fire folkelige Melodier" (Four Popular Melodies) no op., 1925, "Ti danske Smaasange" (Ten Danish Ditties) no op., 1926, (Borup), and "Fire jydske Sange" (Four Jutland Songs) no op., 1941, all of which were published by the music publishers, Wilhelm Hansen, with the exception of the two last collections, which were published by Skandinavisk and Borup's Musikforlag.

There is no collected edition of Nielsen's songs, and many of his songs were only published singly, or in composite works, as the musical accompaniment to plays and other public performances, in cantatas, and so on, indeed, some of his songs have never even been printed. When three or four of his collections of songs had been published, Nielsen lost interest in seeing his compositions appear in the traditional way, catering for professional singers as a kind of invitation to sing them at concerts, or for private performers who likewise considered that songs were for solo performance. With a few exceptions, from then on Nielsen wrote only strophic songs, which both as music and as poems were widely different from the nineteenth century lyrical romance with its dramatic element or its artistic vocal and instrumental strain. It is possible to follow the line which runs through Nielsen's preoccupation with song as a genre, but he did not consciously thread that line through his work, and in fact it is not clearly perceptible until late in his career as a composer.

Characteristically, J. P. Jacobsen was the poet Nielsen chose when he first began to compose songs; this may have been because he had formed the impression that the publication of a book of songs was something a young and struggling composer ought to do. He began to write his solo songs in 1891, and although Jacobsen had then been dead for a number of years, his poems had first become generally known through the posthumous edition "Digte og Udkast" (Poems and Drafts) which was published in 1886, the year after his death. Nielsen was powerfully drawn by the ideas of the circle round the Brandes brothers, and the lucid terseness of the literary radicalism of the day made a far greater impression on him than the swelling rhetoric of Drachmann. Heise just managed to compose the Dyveke-songs by Drachmann in the musical idiom of pre-Impressionism; Nielsen began with Jacobsen's arabesque style which, in poetry, led to poetic symbolism in Denmark. To begin with, the piano accompaniment played an important independent part in his songs, but in calling the first published collection, "Musik til fem Digte af J. P. Jacobsen", Nielsen clearly stresses the equality of words and music.

The appearance of the first collected edition of Jacobsen's poems inevitably made a strong impression on Nielsen, whose mind was so open to everything new that was stirring in the times. Earlier, the great Danish composers of songs had, like Heise, been inspired either by the poets of the Danish Golden Age, such as Christian Winther, Ingemann and Poul Møller in particular, or, like Lange-Müller, by Thor Lange's charming adaptations from Russian folk songs—or by Ernst v. der Recke. It was Jacobsen who first made Nielsen into a singer with a voice which, from the very beginning, had entirely other tonal values than those of both the greater and lesser song writers.

To determine J. P. Jacobsen's greatness as a lyrical poet, it is important to bear in mind that some of his most unusual poems date from as early as the time about 1870. Even in these early poems he had broken away from the accepted metrical forms and had dissolved them into arabesque-like *vers libre*, sometimes almost prose, sometimes veering towards an absolute metrical form, but always fleeing from the average, the mediocre. In his choice of poetic subject Jacobsen is still the Romantic, but his use of imagery and rhythm heralded new ideas.

What was new and progressive in Jacobsen's works came to light in his naturalistic novels and short stories, in which the words gained new life, and in which the rhythm of the language was a direct continuation of the mood he had created in his arabesque lyrics. In Danish poetry this meant the birth of symbolism, and the impression it made on the young generation in the 1890s was enduring. Ludvig Holstein, Viggo Stuckenberg, Johs. Jørgensen, Sophus Claussen, Helge Rode, all of them were more or less of the same age as Nielsen. In Danish music, though for the time being only in Nielsen's music, it meant a stylistic renewal of the song for the piano (which, incidentally, was preceded by the arabesque in "Fem Klaverstykker" op. 3), (Five Pieces for the Piano) whose motto is taken from the opening words of Jacobsen's "Har du faret vild i dunkle skove? Kender du Pan?" (Have you lost your way in the dim woods? Do you know Pan?). The "Fem Digte" (Five Poems) which he set to music as op. 4 and the five following "Viser og Vers" op. 6, were performed together at a concert, in the spring of 1892, and already reveal Nielsen as an innovator in more than one respect. These songs, which were inspired by a poet who became the acknowledged teacher of the lyrical poets of the nineties and of most Danish poets in the next fifty years, far outreached any contemporary Danish songs, both as regards melody and harmony.

In his two volumes of Jacobsen songs Nielsen does in a way continue the song tradition of the Romantic Age. The piano accompaniment plays a very decisive part (this is evident from the title of the first volume, "Music to Five Poems"), and leads the voice far away to distant spheres of harmony which Nielsen only rarely sought in his later songs, and he also lets the mood which the piano part creates as a background for the poems stand out with many characteristic colours. But in the melodic line of the voice itself is augured Nielsen's predilection for simplicity in the use of the interval and for syllabic declamation, an inclination which later became more pronounced. There are many examples of stronger modulation and more chromatic colour in the type of melody which throughout his life was so characteristic of Nielsen's instrumental music, but which is only found in the songs of his youth. The accompaniment may be deeply moved and expressive ("I Seraillets Have"—In the Seraglio Garden) and charmingly ironical ("Genrebillede"—A Genre Picture), and, although the tune may be simple in the extreme, Carl Nielsen rarely denies himself the pleasure of a colourful or strongly impressive accompaniment.

This is particularly pronounced in "Irmelin Rose", where both the tune of the song and the accompaniment follow the text of the poem as closely as possible. In the rather hard, pastiche-like ballad stanzas of this medieval arabesque, with its cheerfully flitting refrain (which underlines and stresses both the situation and the pastiche), Jacobsen has drawn the unfeeling Irmelin, who lets all knights languish for her.

Nielsen immediately caught the metrical contrast and deepened the gulf: first a 'primitive' tune to the main stanza in an A minor key, graduated down and up, accompanied by the piano in unison—as 'medieval' as one could wish—then the refrain following as closely as possible Jacobsen's metrical form. "Irmelin Rose" may be a purely strophic song, but in the next stanzas Nielsen lights up the text with capricious variations. Yet, in the song's ballad-like simplicity, we experience one of the characteristic elements of Nielsen's new-found art.

His preoccupation with songs and poetry in his youth seemed in the beginning to indicate that although he wished to break with the nineteenth century romance tradition, he certainly wished to stay within the limits of the song written for the piano. But already in 1895 he came across "Sang bag Ploven" (Song behind the Plough) in Ludvig Holstein's Poems, and in some strange way this poem inspired him to create a musical form which since held the foremost place in his songs.

The tune he composed for Holstein's poem contains everything that later was to characterize his songs: the firm, broad tune in rounded arches, a predilection for graduated movement, a careful balance between rise and fall, a calm and flowing rhythm. But "Sang bag Ploven" was not intended as a popular song, even less as a patriotic song. Not only does Holstein's text in itself preclude this, but so also do the elements of the melody, the harmony, and the accompaniment.

"Sang bag Ploven" (Song behind the Plough) strikingly synthesizes Nielsens early romance style and the characteristics which were to make him the great innovator of the Danish popular song. The song begins in unison, a very usual feature of Nielsen's songs, and then follows a strongly differentiated chordal accompaniment, in which heavy-treaded slurred quavers in the inner part give the feel of the rhythm of the ploughman's movements and direct the tonal modulations which typify the song. Most of all the strongly effective, gentle colouring of the melody, which is interpreted repeated in the accompanying chords from the dominant C major key to E flat major, where, for a short space, the song comes to rest. Strangely enough, the tune does not entirely fit the text. In this poem, with its wonderfully sensitive and intimate tone, set in the midst of the Danish countryside, Holstein describes the thoughts of the young farmer as he walks behind his plough, dreaming of his young beloved at home; the tune, on the other hand, despite its characteristic features—in particular, the very effective modulated period—seems at once to catch the mood concentrated in the first line of the stanza.

It will thus be realized how fallacious is the present widely accepted assumption that Nielsen did not leave any profound mark on the Danish song until "En Snes danske Viser" I–II, containing contributions by himself and Thomas Laub, appeared in 1915 and 1917. Those features which made him the renewer of the popular Danish song are already evident in his youthful songs for the piano, and even more convincingly in "Sang bag Ploven", and are to be found on and off in the songs he wrote long before he began to collaborate with Laub.

In 1901 he was asked to compose a new tune for Morten Børup's May song, "In vernalis temporis" (Frydeligt med jubelkor) which was to be used for the revival of the traditional Mayday celebration at Kolding Grammar School. Carl

Nielsen composed a tune which may not belong among his very best and which, rhythmically at least, comes very close to the Latin students' song, "Gaudeamus igitur", but in its simplicity and its simple harmony it was a definite step towards a clarity and purity which at that time might be found in a few of the new tunes used in Danish Folk High School circles. But these tunes rarely expressed what the 'proper' composers of the day wished to produce. Some years later, for his own ends, Carl Nielsen composed Jeronimus' song in the opera "Maskarade"; this is certainly a solo song, in fact it has some resemblance to an aria, and indeed it also turns into something of a travesty towards the end, but its whole aim is, after all, popular and—in keeping with the travesty—with a tendency towards philistinism. At the time when he was composing "Maskarade", Carl Nielsen proved in yet a few other songs his ability to compose a compact easily understood diatonic tune. One of these songs, "Du danske Mand" (Thou Danish Man) was composed by request, and the other, "Jens Vejmand" (The Stone-breaker), was included in his last traditional collection of poems, "Strofiske Sange" I—II, which were written between 1903 and 1907 and published in 1907.

The tune to Holger Drachmann's "Du danske Mand", a modern patriotic song, was written for—and somewhat piquantly included in—the Tivoli Summer Theatre revue in 1906; it was a song hit which has achieved a permanent place among Danish songs. Hornemann's tune to L. C. Nielsen's "Vort Hjem, du danske Jord" (Our home, o, Danish earth) from the same year, and the music to Rørdam's "I Sommersol og Blæst" (In summer sun and wind) by the no longer very productive Lange-Müller from the following year deserve to be mentioned in connection with Carl Nielsen's and Drachmann's success. Hornemann's rich and colourful music to the University cantata with the text by L. C. Nielsen for the memorial ceremony on the occasion of King Christian IX's death is far more in the Romantic tradition, while Lange-Müller's seems inspired by Carl Nielsen's 'pure' tone. At all events, it is a far cry from his setting of Drachmann's "Vi elske vort Land" from twenty years before.

Carl Nielsen gradually became aware of the fact that he was able to influence the popular song. Sometimes the popularity which one of his songs would arouse must have left him almost breathless, as when his setting of Jeppe Aakjær's "Jens Vejmand" became a veritable song hit. But he knew what he was capable of. He could thus assure L. C. Nielsen, whose patriotic play "Willemoes" was produced at the Folketeatret in the spring of 1908, "I *will* write a good song, but I will not write a single note before it wells up, quite complete". He kept his promise. The song is known to all Danes to this day: "Havet omkring Danmark" (The Sea around Denmark).

The following years cover the period when Nielsen was conductor of the Royal Theatre orchestra. His compositions from this period are not so numerous, most of them being minor occasional works. He had more than enough to do at the theatre, and was saving his creative energy for the "Sinfonia espansiva", the violin concerto, and the G minor sonata. But hardly had he left the Royal

Theatre before offers, which he would previously have had no time to consider, streamed in. Johan Borup, a well-known Folk High School leader, wanted him to edit the music book for a song book, and Thomas Laub suggested that together they should make a concerted effort on behalf of the Danish song.

Laub would obviously not have suggested this to Nielsen if he had not been absolutely certain of what he was doing. And he had no doubts, because for many years he had seen examples of Nielsen's songs, with their air of artless simplicity, as they appeared, one by one, but full of promise.

Laub and Nielsen had got to know each other early on, as was inevitable for two people who were both involved in the musical life of Copenhagen in the late 1880s and early 1890s, when they both, each in his own way, were regarded as the coming men, Laub in the field of church music, Nielsen in secular music. Their approaches to each other date from the time when Laub, under a storm of protest, had been appointed N. W. Gade's successor as organist at the Holmen's Church, at a time when Nielsen too, was finding difficulty in being understood and accepted. The result was a life-long relationship founded on mutual respect: without completely understanding the intrinsic nature of the other's art they joined hands to the great benefit of that immensely important sphere of Danish music: the popular Danish song. Laub brought with him his intimate knowledge of church music and the medieval folk song, while Nielsen came from the immediate present of music, where he had proved his ability to evolve a popular, simple style, based on his own absorption in the basic elements of the structure of a tune, a style which gained enduring strength from his creative genius.

The extent to which Nielsen had been captivated by Laub's work and theories even before they began to collaborate on the songs is evident from the fact that he, who was no churchman, began to compose hymn tunes. Nielsen must have felt both attracted and perhaps a little repelled by Laub's work, especially perhaps by Laub's own compositions written in the old style. He has clearly recognized the legitimacy of Laub's views and especially Laub's reaction against the use of romances as hymn tunes, but his answer to Laub was a hymn type which contained more subjectively than objectively confessional features. Very few of Nielsen's early hymn tunes are religious in the sense that Laub wished to see. To a certain extent it is true to say of the collected "Salmer og aandelige Sange" (Hymns and Sacred Songs), which finally came out in 1919, that they are more in the nature of community songs than hymns for a congregation. There are some firm compositions among them, but none of them surpass his rendering of Grundtvig's "Min Jesus, lad mit hjerte få en sådan smag for dig" (My Jesus, let my heart find such a taste for Thee), which he later used as the theme of the variation movement of the wind quintet. Laub considered, and in this he was right, that as a composer of hymns Carl Nielsen proved to be no true 'son of the house'. Nevertheless, in the attraction he felt towards the spiritual song, the religious song, was something of the same element which made his secular songs so significant. And on this ground he and Laub gave each other the fullest support and recognition.

124

They found a common denominator in the old songwriter and composer of *singspiele,* J. A. P. Schulz, who, with a delicate and original musical sincerity had lent an air of spirituality to the utilitarian ideal of a song held high by the Age of Reason. Schulz, who is regarded with special veneration in Denmark both because he reorganized the Danish Opera during his stay in Copenhagen in 1787—95 and for his Danish *singspiele,* "Høstgildet" (The Harvest Festival) and "Peter's Bryllup" (Peter's Wedding) so full of melodious tunes, which he wrote during the same period, says in his famous preface to the first volume of his "Lieder im Volkston" that he had tried to give his tunes "das Schein des Bekannten", the touch of the familiar. This element of the apparently well known was also the aim Laub and Nielsen set themselves when, in 1914, they began their collaboration on "En Snes danske Viser" (A Score of Danish Songs), the first volume of which appeared in 1915, followed in 1917 by a further twenty songs or so.

In their own field, these two collections of Danish songs, to be correct, forty-five in all, twenty-three in the first volume, of which twelve were by Nielsen, and twenty-two in the second volume, with eleven by Nielsen, form a central point in modern Danish music, from which strong impulses were radiated not only to other composers but to the whole Danish people. As a nation, the Danes are not particularly fond of singing; perhaps because they have not always had the songs they would like to sing, but in certain happy periods their joy in singing has been re-awakened. Thanks to Laub's and Nielsen's songs, the twentieth century Danish song is a vital and living element in Danish schools, Folk High Schools, and homes.

How this fruitful collaboration came about is described by Nielsen just before the first volume of the songs was published in 1915. It cannot be told more clearly or fully than he himself described it in a letter to the music critic, Gustav Hetsch, who wished to know something about the background of the composition of the songs:

"Laub came to me in November of last year (1914) and suggested that he and I should set to music the songs and poems of some good poets. He said: "If only we could turn the public's taste a hand's breadth towards the simple, the comprehensible, and the purely melodic without lowering the standard, we should win merit for ourselves at a time when songs have more and more become identical with long and difficult piano pieces, where words and tune must often struggle through as best they can." I found this suggestion so good that I immediately agreed to make the attempt. Laub found the poems of our classic poets (Oehlenschläger, Poul Møller, Chr. Winther, Aarestrup, etc.) which had not been set to music, or whose tunes were little known or unsatisfactory—for we had no intention of correcting Gade, Hartmann, Heise, etc. The first tune I composed was to "De Refsnæs Drenge" (The Refsnæs Boys) by Blicher; this was followed by Oehlenschläger's "Underlige Aftenlufte" (Strange Airs of Evening), to which I composed no less than three tunes before we considered that I had caught the right tone of the poem. I know well that both this poem and "Rosen blusser"

(The Rose blossoms) had already been set to music, but as I did not know the tunes, Laub asked me to make the attempt all the same, as in his opinion the existing tunes were not worthy of the poems.—

We have in no way attempted to stylize our tunes; how could we, in the case of Oehlenschläger and Poul Møller, etc.? But I, and I believe this applies equally to Laub, have entered so intensely into the spirit of the poems that in the end it seemed to me that I existed in their world. I suppose we shall be acquitted of the 'old style', which so many present-day composers seem to adore. What do we want with an 'old style' when we have whole mountains of genuinely old and splendid music? Thus, our aim has been to enter into the time and the spirit of the poems without any form of stylization."

It was primarily the marked rhythm and the racily sonorous effect which created the charm of the popular patriotic songs which Nielsen had written before he began to collaborate with Laub in "En Snes danske Viser". In this volume of songs it was the Danish mood or spirit, which through the ages had found its finest and often most intimate expression in Danish poetry, which they wished to express in music. Carl Nielsen had until then read almost exclusively contemporary poetry. When Laub now confronted him with the poems of Blicher, Hans Christian Andersen, Poul Møller, and other Danish poets of the Golden Age of literature and some of Jeppe Aakjær's poems as well, he realized that some of these songs demanded an entirely different, gentle lyrical tone; but Nielsen who had already created some of the finest and purest songs which we possess, e.g. "Du fine hvide Æbleblomst" (Lovely white apple blossom) to the words of Holstein, and "Sænk kun dit Hoved, du Blomst" (Droop now thy head, lovely flower) (Johs. Jørgensen) demonstrated once more his rare gift of creating a mood, only now it was even stronger, more simple, freed of the chromatic colour and of all overstressed modulations. Among these collected songs we find "Underlige Aftenlufte" (Oehlenschläger), "Vender sig Lykken fra dig" (Should happiness turn away from you) (Hauch), and "Nu er Dagen fuld af Sang" (Now is the day full of song) and "Jeg bærer med Smil min Byrde" (With song I bear my burden) by Jeppe Aakjær, all of which form the flower of the new heritage of songs.

In these twenty-odd Danish songs Nielsen was able not only to continue along the course he had already set himself, but he was also to show an even more conscious engrossment in the actual nature of the popular song. And this meant so much to him that for the next ten years he nearly always formed his vocal compositions as simple songs. Only rarely does he deflect from his course, and seriously only twice. The first time was in the idyllic genre piece, "Studie efter Naturen" (Study from Nature) (1916) by Hans Christian Andersen, and the second time was towards the end of this period in the sombre "Ballade om Bjørnen" (Ballad of the Bear) (1923) by Aage Berntsen, adapted from C. J. L. Almquist, in which the dramatic quality of the poem is reproduced in harsh colours. Both the vocal part and the accompaniment are drawn into the descrip-

126

tion. In the abruptness of the vocal lines Nielsen seeks different musical truths than in the songs, and in the accompaniment he makes use of whole complexes of tritone accumulations to stress the horror of the story.

He used the strophic song in his music for Oehlenschläger's play "Aladdin" (1919) and in Helge Rode's play "Moderen" (The Mother) (1921) and in the songs for Danish schools and Folk High Schools.

The first part of the important chapter in Nielsen's life which might be entitled "Carl Nielsen and the Danish Folk High School" was written before Laub and Nielsen began to work together. Johan Borup, who transplanted the Danish Folk High School (which had hitherto been a rural movement) to the urban setting of Copenhagen, in 1914 published a Danish Song book which included a number of contemporary songs. Twenty of them had been set to music by Nielsen, who in 1916 published "Carl Nielsens Melodibog til Johan Borups Sangbog" containing fifteen new songs by himself. In 1918, Pastor Erik Spur, who was connected with Roskilde Folk High School, brought out "Viser og Sange", a collection of one-part songs, including some of Nielsen's which had not previously been published. But the most important event was when, in 1922, after many years of preparation, "Folkehøjskolens Melodibog" (The Folk High School Song Book) saw the light; two young teachers, the composers Thorvald Aagaard and Oluf Ring, had done most of the arduous work of editing this song book, actively assisted by Thomas Laub and Carl Nielsen. About fifty of Nielsen's tunes were included, and this number has remained unchanged throughout the victorious career of this song book in Denmark. Six editions have been issued, and to this day it remains the classic collection of Danish songs of our country, and its influence and use has extended far beyond the Folk High Schools. Shortly afterwards, Nielsen became engaged in a similar campaign to renew the songs used in Danish elementary schools: in 1924 he and the composer Hakon Andersen produced "Melodier til Sangbogen Danmark". Together these two song books have formed the cornerstone of popular singing in Denmark ever since, and practically all subsequent collections of songs are indebted to them.

A number of those songs which Nielsen contributed to "Folkehøjskolens Melodibog" and to "Melodier til Sangbogen Danmark" he also published in "Tyve folkelige Melodier" (1921) and in "Ti danske Smaasange" (1925). Some of them differ from the songs in the song books by having his own piano accompaniment. His piano accompaniment is also more varied than in "En Snes danske Viser", where perhaps Laub's influence is responsible for the often strongly chordal accompaniment. In "Ti danske Smaasange" especially, we encounter the lightly indicated but precise and perfectly effective delicacy of the piano part, quite in the spirit of J. A. P. Schulz, as e.g. in Harald Bergstedt's "Jeg ved en Lærkerede" (I know a lark's nest), where Nielsen equals Schulz' gift of fitting a perfectly round tune to the briefest poetic stanza imaginable. There are other examples of a strictly linear structure of a slight part. In "Ti danske Smaasange", we find this graceful linearity in "Tyst som Aa i Engen rinder" (Silent as a brook through the meadow flows) (Helge Rode) and particularly in "Jeg lægger mig saa trygt til Ro" (I lie down so peacefully to rest) (Chr. Winther) which continues the two-part theme from "Hvor sødt i Sommeraftenstunden" (How sweetly in the summer evening) (Oehlenschläger) from "En Snes danske Viser", Volume II. Even in this very slight form it is possible to find echoes of his earliest songs for the piano, such as "Grøn er Vaarens Hæk" (Green is the hedge in spring) (Poul Møller).

Yet another collection of songs, "Nye Melodier til Borups Sangbog", with thirteen new songs by Carl Nielsen, appeared in 1926, but this was also the end of a contribution to Danish music no less valuable than that which Nielsen rendered to serious music. He broke off when he felt that his mission was complete and then let others continue along the beaten paths—even to the stagnation of this musical genre. He probably felt that he was unable to express much more in the strophic song than he had already done, and he was forced to recognize that not everything that he had created in this sphere of music was fated to survive for ever. Several of Nielsen's songs have not stood the test of time; he lived to realise that the strength of his name was not enough to save from oblivion some of the things he had written, which was perhaps the greatest compliment that popular taste and praise could have paid to his real masterpieces *en miniature*. On the other hand, the best of his popular songs have something which made them acceptable to the whole people, and which raised them high above the currents of fashion. Very few composers have had the fortune to have fifty songs accepted by the people, and which have remained in their affection.

There was other work for him to do; new impulses from the music which was sounding in the Europe of the post-war years caught his imagination, he who was always so receptive. On rare occasions he returned to the Danish song, but otherwise he trod quite new paths in the great works of his later years: the sixth symphony, the flute concerto, and particularly the clarinet concerto; the three pieces for the piano, the three motets for a cappella choir, and the keystone of his creative genius, the organ composition "Commotio".

(Translated by Ellen Branth)

INDEX OF WORKS CITED

DATE DUE
